Upside Down

and

Other Stories

Edited by

JULIA T. LYE

DeeBee

Upside Down and Other Stories

Copyright © 2020 by DeeBee Books

For information contact David Allan Hamilton:
davidallanhamilton00@gmail.com
www.deebeebooks.com

Layout by Léa Marshall-Raymond
Cover art by TBD

ISBN: 9781896794389

First Edition: August, 2020

10 9 8 7 6 5 4 3 2 1

CONTENTS

The Legend of Green Snake and White Snake

By Wanying Zhang

HER SLANTED BROWN EYES APPEAR TO GLOW AS SHE STARES INTO the snow-capped mountain peaks in the distance. Her black hair, held up by a single clip, tumbles down her back in a dark cascade. A simple white dress drapes her elegant figure. She gazes like that into the distance for hours. Time flows like water in a creek. Green Snake admires her from a distance. She desires a body like White Snake's someday. Green Snake has been training studiously every day, so she can summon enough magic to turn into a human. White Snake is about a thousand years older than she is. White Snake's human form is flawless, with not even a hint of the serpentine in her demeanor. Green Snake has been observing her for several years now, always too shy to approach her. This is White Snake's favorite spot; she comes here to be alone and to think.

The day of the first snowfall, Green Snake reluctantly goes into hibernation. She envies White Snake for not having to hibernate in her human form. Green Snake tells herself that she will dream about White Snake and see her in the spring and be more beautiful than ever. Green Snake feels that she is close to achieving her transformation. One more year, Green Snake thinks to herself, and she will be able to transform into a human and approach White Snake in person.

***

A SHIVER RUNS DOWN WHITE SNAKE'S SPINE as the first snowflake of the season lands on her nose. Still dressed in a thin white dress, she descends from her favorite outlook where she contemplates humans and their nature. White Snake tries to integrate into human society; she tries to be one of them. She names herself Bai, a human name. She uses her magic to perform acts of kindness, especially for healing. One day, with the sun raging above like a hot furnace, she encounters a young man who walks with a purposeful stride. He carries a heavy hiker's backpack full of books and his brow glistens with sweat as he traverses a dangerous, slippery road along the cliff. Curious, she follows him from afar. He makes a false step and slips, twisting his ankle. His books scatter on the dirty ground. He stumbles to catch a book that is on the edge of the cliff. In his haste, the book falls and he loses his balance. Bai flies towards him and catches him

3

just as he is about to fall to his death.

***

GREEN SNAKE GROGGILY AWAKENS FROM HER SLUMBER. The fresh smell of wet grass permeates her den. She ought to have a place more suitable for a human. She looks at her green scaly body and feels even more determined to get rid of this wretched body. The image of White Snake appears in her mind like a distant dream. She remembers the first time she met White Snake, a couple hundred years ago...

Green Snake was sunbathing on a rock, minding her own business, when a human hand came down on her. The next thing she knew she was in darkness and she couldn't move very far in any direction without encountering impenetrable walls. It dawned on Green Snake that she had been imprisoned.

Green Snake was trapped for what must have been hours before she heard an airy female voice.

"I would like to buy that green snake from you." The woman with the airy voice offered.

"How did you know I captured a green snake?" the merchant asked, puzzled.

"I saw you pick it up from the road a while back. I happen to need it for some medicine. Would you accept my humble offer to buy it off of your hands?" The merchant didn't ask further questions. He handed over Green Snake to the woman with the airy voice. Green Snake had felt terrified inside her dark prison but the thought of being turned into medicine terrified her even further. Then the woman spoke to Green Snake.

"Here you are, little snake, I set you free. I hope you live well." She released her into the safety of the scrubby undergrowth. Green Snake had felt the woman's blood resonate with hers when they touched. She looked into her eyes and they had a moment of mutual understanding. At that time, Green Snake realized that she must become like the woman, so Green Snake could be with her and have the same power over humans. Thus, Green Snake would be able to repay the woman properly for her kindness.

The frost on the trees is just beginning to melt as the morning sun kisses their tips. Green Snake heads to White Snake's favorite spot, her heart beating with excitement to see White Snake again after a long hibernation. But, as White Snake comes into view, Green Snake's excitement is replaced with a sinking feeling. Wrapped in her arms is a man. He seems insignificant and mortal. But White Snake never brings anyone else to her favorite spot. What is so special about this mortal?

I'm too late, Green Snake thinks. Green Snake wanted to be there for White Snake, but someone else had taken her place.

"I know what you're thinking," a small voice speaks. Green Snake whips her head around.

"Who's there?"

"Over here, I'm hanging from a branch." Green Snake scans her surroundings until her eyes narrow on a speckled spider the size of an apple hanging from a single gossamer thread. The spider looks quizzically at Green Snake with her many eyes, her eight elegant legs arranged symmetrically in a diamond. "You want to become human like her. You want to be with her."

"How do you know?"

"Please, I have been a spider for hundreds of years. I can see the look in your eyes, even if you are still just a snake."

"Can you help me then?"

"Perhaps. I do know a quicker way."

"Really? Is it some magic elixir?"

"Nothing that fancy. It's dark magic."

"What do you mean?"

"You have to suck a human soul. Of course, you can stick with your regular training to become human. But if you want a shortcut then this is the best solution. Each human soul will give you an extra tenfold of magic."

"How do you know?"

"My dear, I did it myself! I was like you trying to become human the straight and narrow way, but then one day I accidentally took a human soul and just like that, I could turn into a human. Ever since then, I have never looked back."

"Show me."

The little spider drops to the ground and instantly transforms into a lady just as beautiful as White Snake. Her black gown bears the same speckled pattern as her spider's body. She picks up Green Snake with one hand and rests her on her shoulder.

"Believe me now little one?"

"That's unbelievable, you're a perfect human!"

"We can help each other. I can easily capture a human for you, but you have to get me a serpent's egg."

"An egg? Why do you want an egg?"

"That is none of your concern. I get you a human, you get me an egg and I'll show you how to suck his soul. Deal?" Green Snake feels a flutter of unease but she agrees.

***

BAI FEELS SOMETHING SHE HASN'T FELT BEFORE. The human that she rescued tells her of his dreams and aspirations, piquing her curiosity. He shows her his favorite book, *Journey to the West*.

"Where were you going with all those books?" She inquires.

"I was headed to take the state exam. If I pass, I may be able to become a noble and bring in enough money for my aging father and hopefully do justice for the citizens of our town."

"That's kind of you. I'm always looking for places to help people in need. Guess that's how I met you." She smiles.

"But how did you know I was in trouble?"

"Let's just say I have an intuition for these things. I just like helping people."

***

GREEN SNAKE SLITHERS BACK TO HER DEN and steals one of her cousin's eggs. Her cousin lays a new egg every year and Green Snake figures that her cousin will get over losing this one egg. Green Snake presents the stolen egg to the spider lady, who seems deeply satisfied.

"What are you going to do with it?" asks Green Snake.

"As I said, it's none of your concern. I have captured a nice juicy human for you."

She brings the green snake on her arm to one of her caves covered with spider webs, and bundled in a tangle of webs is a wide-eyed man with silk webs stuffed in his mouth.

"This is it?"

"Yes, now the first step is the kill. I saved that part for you as the one who makes the kill must take his soul."

"I have to kill him?"

"Why, of course! How else do you expect to take his soul?" Green Snake looks sympathetically at the man and she freezes in place.

"Come on! Don't tell me you're backing out now. It's for that pretty White Snake, right? If it makes you feel better, I really only capture the scumbags of the earth. You know, the men who like to look at women the wrong way."

Green Snake still hesitates. She wonders what White Snake would think of her if she ever found out. But then again, she might never have the chance to be with White Snake if she doesn't become a human. Green Snake

7

slithers over to the human, takes one last look at him and sinks her teeth into his neck. There is no sign of struggle, but his eyes glaze over and his body goes limp.

"Atta girl! Your first kill, I presume? Don't worry. It gets easier after the first one. It will be like capturing food." The spider lady says flippantly. "Now, after the kill, you have to be quick so that the soul doesn't escape. While the flesh is still soft, dig your teeth into his heart and you should feel the remaining life flickering away inside him. That's the energy you want to take, and transfer it into you. Once you feel that energy transfer, you can rip his heart out and eat it. It's as simple as that."

"You didn't tell me it was that gruesome!"

"You want the soul or not? Time's a-wasting." Green Snake doesn't have much time to think, so she does what the spider lady says. As Green Snake sinks her teeth into the man's body, she feels a surge of energy unlike anything she has felt before. With a single jerk of her head, she rips out the man's heart and swallows it whole. Blood dripping from her mouth, her entire snake skin tingles as if it was on fire. She whispers the incantation to turn human. Her body trembles as bones form inside and crack into place. Her snake skin sheds away behind her as her new skin stretches over her body. Black hair sprouts from her head and tumbles down her back. She lands on all fours, unsure how to walk on her new legs. She stretches her hands out in front of her, looking at her elegant nails for the first time. She cries tears of joy.

***

BAI GOES TO HER FAVOURITE SPOT AND IS SURPRISED to see another woman standing there with her back turned. The woman's black hair tousles gently in the wind. She wears a long, emerald green dress that drapes down her body. Her eyes search the distance as she straightens her back. Sensing no malice, Bai approaches her.

"I like to come here to think as well," Bai says gently from behind her. Green Snake turns around and her heart soars upon seeing her, but she contains her excitement.

"Yes, I know, I have been watching you."

"Have you? I see we're the same kind, have we met before?"

"Yes, I owe you gratitude. I was that green snake you saved a few years ago."

Bai racks her memories. "Ah yes, I remember now. If you came to pay me back, I don't need anything in return," Bai offers.

"I would still like to pay my gratitude, after all a debt of life is not one to take lightly."

"It's not a big deal, really. It's kind of what I do. I look for people or creatures in trouble so I can help them."

"How noble of you. I admire you, so if you would accept me, I would like to learn from you."

"Hmm, well, I suppose I could use a friend. I haven't encountered too many snakes that evolved to be human in these recent lifetimes. I am glad to have met you."

"Likewise."

"I take it you don't have a human name. Should I give you one?"

"That's a nice idea, what do you suggest?"

"Well given that you are a green snake, how about Spring?"

"Spring. I like that name."

"You can call me Bai."

✳✳✳

Spring feels triumphant and joyous as she returns home to her den. Flicking her tongue, she tastes the air in her deteriorating snake den. The sound of dank water dripping from the low ceiling echoes. She wants to demolish this filthy den of hers and build herself a nice home fit for a human. She smells the musty odour of wet wood and damp grass as the many snakes slither over one another like tangled knots. The home she has known her entire life now feels suffocating.

"My daughter, what's troubling you?" Green Snake's mother inquires as she coils up.

"I want to build us a nice home so we don't have to live in the wild anymore. We will be more protected."

"My dear, I have lived in this den for generations and your sisters and brothers have as well. I have no wish to live in a human home."

"We've lived in fear for centuries, hunted by creatures and humans alike. Sometimes we can't even have enough food for everyone. I'm sick of this life."

"Be that it may, Greenie, this is still our home. And I will not uproot our family for the sake of your wild fantasies."

"But I am a human now mother, I can make our lives better. I have met someone and I want to be with her. And I have the power to protect you now."

"Greenie, that is your business. I do not wish to move with you. I hope you can reconsider as well. Don't forget that you are a snake. You can draw the veil of magic and pretend to be human all you want, but you are still a snake. This is our way of life."

"I know who I am, mother. I just believe that I finally met someone worthy of my time. I won't force you to move, but don't say I didn't offer."

Her mother shakes her scaly head and retreats back into the den. If her mother doesn't want to rebuild their den, then Spring will find a home within the humans' village.

***

SHE WANDERS AROUND WITHOUT LUCK, as she quickly realizes that everything in the human world requires money. Finally, Bai spots her and offers to put her up. Spring is deeply grateful. When she enters Bai's home, she is surprised to find that the human she saw with Bai is at her place as well.

"Who is this?" Spring whispers to Bai.

"He is a friend." Bai explains. "I met him on the road and was extending my hospitality to him as he has injured himself from a nasty fall." In a lower voice she adds, "He does not know our true nature so do not reveal your snake form in front of him. I'm afraid it will scare him."

Green Snake looks up and down at him curiously. He does not look injured any longer. He gives Bai an inquiring look.

"He still needs a place to stay, so I offered. It's nice to have some company." Spring sees the look in Bai's eyes and feels a pang of jealousy.

***

A SENSE OF KINSHIP GROWS BETWEEN BAI AND SPRING as they cohabitate. Bai's home is a cozy, well-decorated home with a warm hearth and thick walls for insulation. She had built it herself, living alone for many years, but it feels more like home now. Finally, someone of her kind she can talk to and understand, she was grateful for their sisterhood. At the same time, she feels a magnetic pull towards the human.

"Are you sure you can trust him?" Spring asks.

"Sure, why not?"

"I just heard stories about men, especially male travelers. They can take advantage of you."

"Don't worry my friend, I have magic. I have gotten to know him for a while, he puts his studies first. He's different. He treats every living creature and human with kindness and never expects anything in return. We share the same sense of altruism. Even if I live like a mortal for his sake, if anything happens I can always use magic to protect me."

"Do you... like him... I mean *that* way?"

Bai ponders for a moment before answering, "I think I do, yes. But it's complicated as creatures of another species, we cannot like a human. It's well, I suppose, against nature."

"Then what are you going to do?"

"I'm not sure. He has to leave soon to take his state exam." Soon enough, he departs to start his journey again. He said he will come back to visit her when the state exam is over.

Bai feels a sense of longing she has never felt before.

***

SPRING FEELS RELIEVED THAT SHE CAN BE WITH BAI alone at last. Weeks pass by in perfect harmony as they spend hours chatting about their lives and experiences. One summer day, on their daily stroll while the sun is high in the sky, they hear shouting coming from inside a run-down home, held together by scraps of wood and cloth. Spring peeks in and sees a man beating his wife.

Spring prepares to strike a deadly blow with magic. But Bai held up her hand, blocking Spring's move.

"No, that's not the right way."

Bai casts her magic and sends the man flying backwards. The wife looks at him, bewilderment written on her face. Bai then reveals herself.

The man looks at the figure emerging from the shadows as he witnesses the beautiful woman transform into a gigantic white snake with fangs. She issues her warning.

"If I ever see you beat your wife again, I will personally come and eat you." The little bald man, rendered speechless, faints. The wife thanks them as they leave.

***

"Is IT DIFFICULT LIVING AS A HUMAN FOR SO LONG?" Spring asks when they reach home. She absentmindedly picks at her long hair, a new habit she has picked up in her human form.

"Depends on how you look at it. To be honest, I've inhabited my human form for so long, that I sometimes forget that I'm a snake. It's so easy to blend in with this body and it gives a certain power over people. But sometimes, it can be liberating to be a snake again."

"What's it like for you after all these years?"

"Time passes like sand I suppose. I watch people age and die, I see the laughter of children and the love in their eyes, but I also see their darkest nature when the world turns its cold back on them. I can't stay in one place too long unless I am discovered. It is a bit lonely at times, I have no family left. You are my new family. I have to be cautious not to reveal my true nature to others." Bai starts cutting some vegetables and throwing them in an iron cast wok. She kindles the fire below with some wood.

"I see. I thought the world of humans was a beautiful place where they didn't have the same problems as us." Spring watches the fire crackle to life.

"The world is a complex place," Bai says as if to a child. "The humans have their own sufferings and joys. But their world changes every day, sometimes it's hard to keep up."

"There's so much, it is overwhelming at times," Spring adds, "Do you think they will ever accept us if they knew? I mean, did you look at the way that man looked at you?"

"It's hard to say, I don't have an answer for that."

"Is that why you don't use magic unless necessary? Not even for cooking?" She gestures to the stove.

"It's not worth the risk being discovered, and besides, not everything is satisfying when done by magic." Silence stretches between them as the fire under the stove continues its steady burn.

"You know, for a long time, I always felt beneath everyone. Even my own mother never believed in me. Humans detest snakes. They take our skin and make money out of them. To them, we are just a commodity. I thought being human would be different."

"You're right Spring, but there is not much we can do. It's hard to change human nature."

"But we can eliminate the ones who wrong us." The flame dances in her eyes as she traces over Bai's figure, longing to touch her... to hold her.

"It's not that simple. I was once like you, Spring. But sometimes we just have to settle for just doing what we can in the world for the good of everyone. I just hope I do enough well in the world to achieve divinity."

***

AFTER DINNER, BAI RETIRES TO HER ROOM AND SPRING decides to take an evening stroll. She walks along the same path they walked this afternoon and passes the home where the man beat his wife. To her dismay, she hears again shouting and screaming and she feels that what Bai did was not enough. She slips inside as a snake and indeed hears the torrent of insults thrown at the wife.

"You dirty woman, what unholy business have you been dealing with to bring such magic into our home!? I should have you hanged you for this."

The woman, in tears, her hair a tangled mess, looks more distraught than this afternoon. Fresh bruises colour her arms like purple flowers. She pleads, "No, I haven't done anything. I'm only your wife, you have to believe me!"

Spring has heard enough of this. She sneaks up behind the man and bites his foot. The little man screams in agony and the woman continues crying.

"What black magic is this? Are you calling snakes to kill me?"

The woman shakes her head. Spring grows bigger until she is as tall as the human.

"We told you to leave her alone!"

He tries to swipe at her but misses. Spring sinks her fangs into his throat as images of her first kill play in her mind, but she remembers the spider's words. She tears out the man's heart and feels another surge of magic flow through her. The woman howls with terror in the corner of the shack.

"What have you done?" She says.

"I got rid of him for you. You should thank me."

"He was my husband. I still love him."

"Even with how he treated you?" She looks closer and realizes that the woman isn't completely human either. She was a rabbit spirit living as a human. Their eyes locked with understanding.

"He wasn't always like this. I thought he would understand my true nature, so I told him. I didn't think he would turn this way. But after we ran into some financial trouble, he started to get bitter and then would blame me. I tried to please him, but he said I was a terrible wife and he thought that we were cursed, because of who I am..." She weeps.

"You are better off without him." Spring replies. She can't think of anything else to tell the rabbit spirit. Before she leaves, she uses her magic to fix the broken walls and worn down furniture in the home. The rabbit spirit neither notices nor acknowledges the transformations. So Spring returns home to Bai. Spring thinks it would be best that Bai didn't know about what Spring had just done. But one thing the spider said was right. After the first kill, it doesn't feel as bad anymore.

***

SPRING MELTS INTO SUMMER AND THE TREES regain their foliage. The human keeps his word and returns to Bai. He comes to propose marriage as he has successfully passed the state exam and will be initiated to become a minister very soon. Bai isn't prepared for this. She asks him to give her three days to think.

"Are you sure you want to go through with this?" Spring asks at a last attempt to sway her. "You will have to give up magic, perhaps permanently."

"I can still help people without magic."

"But you will be living with a mortal. He will age and you will not. How are you going to keep your secret very long?"

"I will tell him eventually, when the time is right."

"Do you think he will handle it well?" Spring asks, thinking of the abusive man and his wife. She was afraid for Bai and at the same time didn't want her in somebody else's arms.

"I have faith in him. I care about him and he cares about me. That should be enough. I know you're worried and you are like a sister to me. Nothing will change that."

Spring chews on Bai's optimism, but she doesn't share the same faith. The last thing Spring wants to see is Bai getting hurt, thus she must handle the situation with tact.

Spring goes to forage for some herbs that are known to lower inhibitions. They are especially potent to snakes, as they will make them dizzy and unaware of their surroundings. She grinds these herbs into powder and mixes them into the soup that she has prepared for Bai. The three of them sit down for dinner around the round table as Spring presents them the meal with only Bai's soup drugged. They all eat and drink with gusto.

"I'm not sure I feel too good," Bai says suddenly halfway through the meal. "I think I will go lie down."

"Oh dear, let me help you to bed." The human expresses concern for her, which makes Spring feel uncomfortable. She suppresses her feelings and feigns concern as well.

"It's alright, I think I just had a long day," Bai said.

"It's no trouble." The human insists, already helping to lift her up from the chair. Spring watches him support Bai into the bedroom before following behind. Bai's aura fades in and out, and glimpses of her scales begin to show on her skin.

"What's wrong my love? Your skin feels so cold."

Bai realizes what is happening and her eyes widened in fear.

"Honey, I--I just need to be alone right now, can you please leave?"

"Are you sure? You look pale. You're turning all white."

"Ye-ess." She says weakly.

"I can't leave you like this."

Bai grunts in pain as more scales climb over her skin. She pushes the human away, desperate to hide from him. He stands there dumbfounded. Bai is unable to hold her human form any longer and with a painful gasp, she transforms into a white snake. The human watches the scene unfold as his eyes bulge out in horror. He faints to the floor.

***

BAI AWAKENS THE NEXT DAY, COILED IN HER SNAKE FORM. She transforms easily back into her human form and sees the human lying on the floor. She gently shakes him awake, nervous of his reaction to her. He wakes up bleary eyed and disorientated.

"What happened?" he asks.

"I think you fainted."

"Oh, I had the most terrible dream. I dreamt that you... you were a snake and that you were cold and had fangs ... Oh it was horrible."

Bai stays silent for a while.

"It wasn't a dream…"

"I'm sorry?"

"I--I am actually a snake."

Now it was his turn to stay silent. He stares bewildered at his fiancé.

"What do you mean? You're the most beautiful and kind woman I've ever met, how can you be a snake?"

"I can show you… Just please don't be shocked again?" He nods, his eyes never leaving her. She transforms into a white snake again and looks up at him. He gapes, but stands solid as a stone. Within a minute, she transforms back into a human. "I'm sorry that I kept it from you. I didn't want to scare you."

"This is a lot to process…"

"I know… I understand if you change your mind about us and about taking me as your wife…" Bai turns away, looking at the floor. To her surprise, he takes her hand.

"Bai, I have never loved anyone before like the way I love you. So what if you are a snake, I will still love you all the same."

Bai let out a sigh of relief that she didn't know she had been holding.

***

SPRING'S PLAN TO REVEAL BAI'S NATURE HAS BACKFIRED. She had hoped that he would run away in fear when he saw Bai as a snake and Bai would be all hers. But since they passed this trial of love, she had no choice but to watch them get married. Like a good sister, she blessed their union, keeping her love a secret. They moved into the city, where there were more people and more interesting smells in the air. Bai opened up a modest medicine shop and her husband went on to become a minister. Spring watched Bai seal away her magic so she would not be tempted to use it. She tried not to watch them happily enjoy themselves, but she couldn't help but picture herself in his place. There must be another way than waiting for this human to age and die. She has already waited a few hundred years for her, this man was merely a small obstacle. Still, she must handle this delicately. Spring has ripped out a number of human hearts recently and sucked out their souls. She was careful to pick people who didn't have family or were doing wrong to others. A priest had been hired by the city-dwellers to investigate, as the gruesome killings were clearly not the work of a human. She overheard the human talking to Bai.

"I have a plan," The human tells her eagerly. "I want to help the people who are less fortunate build more houses on the edge of the city, so they can live in better conditions and with better security. The village that you used to live in seems quiet and safe. Maybe it would quell their fear of demons. It could be good for my father as well."

"That is a generous idea. Let me know what I can do to help."

"Maybe it's best if you stay at home more..."

"What do you mean?"

"Well, you wouldn't want people to get suspicious of well... your nature," he says hesitantly.

"You're not saying you think I had something to do with this do you?"

"No, no not at all! I'm just worried what others' reaction might be if they found out."

"Since when do you care what others think?"

"I'm the minister now, I have certain responsibilities and a reputation to uphold," he tries explaining.

"Well, you haven't told anyone right? Then it should be fine. I have lived many lifetimes before without being discovered. I think I can handle myself." Bai stalks away, and Spring smiles to herself behind the door.

***

BAI'S HUSBAND DOESN'T TALK TO HER FOR A WHILE. She hopes that she wasn't too harsh on him. She commits herself to some embroidery to distract herself. A harsh knock comes to the door. She opens the door to a man wearing a hood staring at her coldly.

"May I help you?"

"Be gone, demon!" he yells as he holds up a lantern that lights up as he nears it towards her.

"What are you doing? I'm not a demon! Husband!"

Bai's husband comes from behind the kitchen as he witnesses his wife being subdued.

"Stay back my brother! I am trying to save your soul, she has seduced you! Your house has been invaded by a demon!"

"I'm no demon! I'm his wife! Tell him dear!" Her husband is at loss for words. She pleads with him with her eyes.

"No one can save you! Your union is against nature! You cannot stay here, I have to take you away!"

"No please! I haven't done anything!"

Bai couldn't summon her magic as she had sealed it away. The priest holds her arm with a strong grasp and murmurs something under his breath while holding out a mini figurine of a pagoda tower the size of his hand. She finds herself shrinking smaller and smaller, and then blackness descends upon her.

***

SPRING VISITS HER MOTHER AT HER DEN near the village that she used to stay in. She wrinkles her nose at the state of the den as the smell is more acute to her as a human and again wonders why her mother would subject herself to such conditions. She transforms back into a snake and slithers inside, but she doesn't expect to see the den mostly abandoned. The aroma of smoke and burnt insects taints the air.

"What happened? Where did everyone go?" she asks.

"Greenie! You came back. You haven't heard? The humans are going to build houses on our land. We were forced to evacuate."

"What? Are you sure? You didn't fight back?"

"What can we do, Greenie? The humans overwhelmed us. They burned our home. Some of us died." Spring notices a patch of burnt skin on her mother's scales. She realizes what she has done.

"I'm sorry mother. I will try to fix this. Try to find somewhere safe for now."

"Greenie!" Spring slips away and transforms back into a human. She vows that she will never forget again that she is a snake.

***

WHEN SPRING COMES BACK, SHE FINDS THAT BAI IS GONE. She interrogates the human and he confesses what happened. At night, she goes to seek out the miniature pagoda tower in which Bai has been imprisoned. She slithers into the temple where the priest resides and finds the tower resting on a corner table like an ornament. Her heart thumps louder than she thought was possible as a snake. She transforms herself so that she is small enough to enter the tower. She kicks open the door and finds Bai behind enchanted bars.

"What did they do to you?" Spring exclaims.

"They locked me up. Thank god you're here! Please help me!" Spring tries to cast magic on the bars, but they remain unaffected.

"It's not working! I think it's magic proof!" Spring says desperately.

"What am I going to do? My husband must be really worried right now." Bai replies, her eyes scanning her prison, unable to focus on anything.

"You're locked in a tower, and all you can think about is him?"

"What else would I think about?" Bai snaps.

"Oh, I don't know. How to get out of here?"

"How did they find out what I am? I don't understand! I have been so careful for centuries..." After a long silence, she says, "Do you think my husband told him of my nature? You have to tell the priest, I didn't do anything!"

"I know you didn't do anything to deserve this... but I did. This is all my fault."

"What are you talking about?"

"I stirred up fear in the city, including in your husband. I took away the criminals and loners in the city. I wanted to finish what you were too cowardly to do!" cried Spring. "You gave up all your magic and power for a mere human. He's not worth it."

"No, it can't be! Tell me you're lying!"

"It's true, Bai. I couldn't stand seeing you with a simple human. You just settle and open some medicine shop, turn away from magic and pretend to play human. You have so much potential! I can't watch you give up your dream of divinity."

"It is my choice! What do you have against him?"

"I'll have you know, he wants to build houses over our snake den and destroy who knows what other animal's homes. I can't let him do that. Where would my family go? He may seem nice to you today, but he will change... he has changed."

"What do you mean? He wanted to build them for the less fortunate people. It wasn't his intention to destroy your den."

"No, you forget that you are a snake! Stop defending him! Some of your kin has died because of him. He chose the location because it was more profitable and remote. Think about it, it was a well sunlit area, next to downstream water. But we were living there for centuries. He wouldn't have thought of the idea if it weren't for me stirring up unrest in the village."

"There must have been some sort of mistake!" Bai pushes back her tears.

"I tried to protect you from the truth, Bai. I really don't want to see you get hurt! But you defend them like you are one of them! And look what they did to you!"

"Some things are worth the sacrifice…"

"You want to talk about sacrifice? Remember when we were in the village and it was just the two of us doing good deeds? Well, I killed the dirt bags you couldn't kill, so you didn't have to sully your hands! You think you can do justice by weaving some magic and people will then listen to you? People don't! I drugged your soup, hoping he would leave when he saw your true nature. And I was the one who gave an anonymous tip to the priest that there was a demon living amongst us, not your husband. I did all this for you."

"What!? You did all of that? How could you!?" Bai's accusing look burns into Spring's eyes as the edges of her words cut deep into her heart. "You shouldn't have killed any people!" She grips the bars so tight that her knuckles turn white.

"I tried being nice, Bai. I really tried, but people will just step all over you and I'll be treated just like another snake to be kicked aside or another woman to be left behind. I already lived like that for centuries as a snake. I wanted to live differently as a human."

"Why? Why did you do this for me? You could have just left me alone, and we wouldn't be in this mess."

"Because… you deserve better."

"What are you trying to say?"

"I did all this because… because… I love you!"

Bai stays silent for a while.

"I love you. There I said it! Not just like a sister, I love you, I dreamt about being with you the first moment I met you."

"You never said anything." Bai said quietly. "I'm not sure what to say…

24

I don't think I can love you that way. I love him… and I don't think I can love anyone else the same way I love him. I know he may have wronged you, I'm sorry. I didn't realize that you did so much for me, but I never asked for any of it!"

Spring feels her heart crack into pieces as Bai's words hit her blow by blow. She knew all along the truth was right in front of her, but she had hung on to the hope that they could still be together. "Please. Just let me go. I just want to talk to him… to see him."

"I know you didn't ask for any of this. I'm sorry… I really am. I just wanted my own chance at happiness. But now I see we're too different. I can't sit here and pretend to be as nice as you and do things the 'right way.' I really thought I could be a real human, but I was wrong. I can wear this human skin and talk like one of them but I will always be a snake."

"Spring, I love you like a sister and I don't want to harm you either. There's still time to turn back."

"You really love him, don't you?" Spring asks in resignation. She sees the answer in Bai's eyes. "I'll see what I can do."

Spring runs away from the pagoda tower, tears streaming down her face as the reality hits her. She seeks out the spider for help.

***

"I HAVE TO FIX SOMETHING. I SCREWED UP," Spring confesses to the spider.

"Well, well look who it is, Green Snake has finally grown up. I see you have sucked many more souls… how does it feel to be on the dark side?"

"No, I don't want to be! I did all this for Bai! I just want to fix it."

"Whatever you say, little snake. You can't undo what's already been done."

"A priest locked up Bai in a magic-proof tower and I have no way to break her free. And my den has been destroyed! I was hoping maybe you can help me."

"You still want to help her, even though she still loves the human?"

"How did you know?"

"I know things, Greenie."

"Can you help?"

"Of course... but for a price."

"Let me guess, you want another egg?"

"Correct, my friend. I can easily subdue this priest of yours, but after all it is work."

"Will you tell me what you did with the first egg?"

"I ate it," the spider snickered. "It gives me a hundredfold worth of magic power compared to a human's soul."

"You're sick!"

"You handed it to me. Face it, you're just like me now. In this world, I'd rather kill than be killed."

"Well, I don't have another egg, half our family got destroyed. I can't afford to give you one even if we had one. What else do you want from me?"

"Well there is something...."

"Fine. Tell me what I should do."

***

GREEN SNAKE PUTS ON HER BEST DRESS, making sure to show a little skin and seeks out the priest. She makes sure she wears the pendant that the spider gave her so the priest won't detect her nature.

"Hello there," she says seductively. The priest turns his head in surprise at her voice. "I have a little surprise for you."

"Oh?"

"I was the one who left the note that there was a demon, but there is more... I know where they are and I can show you. Imagine if you capture them, all the credit will go to you."

"Really? Do tell... but why are you telling me?"

"I'm just a village girl who cares about the safety of her neighbors and I know you are the one who can do it."

"Indeed. We must capture those demons and put them in their place!"

"Of course, but I can't tell you here. There are too many ears. It's best if I show you."

The priest brings his pagoda tower and follows Spring to the edge of the city where trees line the horizon.

"They are in the forest?"

"Of course, demons don't come out in broad daylight. They like to stay in the shadows. What better place than the forest?" The priest nods in agreement.

The spider has recreated her nest and hung endless webs from all of the trees. The priest seems to get more nervous with every step.

"Here it is..." Spring whispers. They stand in front of the mouth of a cave covered with spider webs.

"How many of them are in there? I may need more back up."

"Don't bother... it's too late." A female voice comes from inside. The spider lady emerges from the darkness twice as big as the human himself and looks at him with her many eyes.

The priest, frozen in place, is too scared to act. He reaches for his pagoda tower, but the spider is quicker. She spits a web onto his face to seal his mouth. With two of her legs she picks him up like a toy soldier and starts wrapping him in her web. The tower falls out of his hands as he grows dizzy from being spun at such speed. The spider is about to go for the kill, but Spring stops her.

"Wait! Don't kill him yet, we need to know how to unlock the tower." Spring says.

The spider throws the human violently into one of her webs where he is unable to move any limbs.

"You heard her. Unlock the tower." The wide-eyed priest did nothing.

"Looks like you need some motivation." As the spider lady prepares to strike, he starts to make some muffled sounds.

"I think he's trying to speak," Spring says. The spider lady rips the web from his mouth.

"Speak!" she commands.

"I have the-the key! It needs a key and an ancient code to open. Please don't hurt me!"

"Where's the key?"

"In my pocket." Spring fishes out the key. The metal lays heavy in her hand.

"And the code?"

"Will you let me go?"

"Only if you disappear, and never come back." He nods in agreement and tells them the code.

***

"YOU FREED ME. THANK YOU." Spring and Bai's husband stand at the entrance of the temple waiting for her. Spring brings the pagoda tower back to the temple and unlocks the tower.

"No, thank you. You saved me from myself."

"I'm sorry I ever doubted you," her husband adds. "Spring explained everything to me." Bai looks at her husband lovingly. Spring looks away.

The spider emerges from the temple as a human. She is cocooned in her signature black dress and its ends billows in the wind. She licks her dark lips as she stands in front of them expectantly.

"Who's this?" Bai asks.

"Well, I see Spring has not mentioned me. I have to say, Spring, I'm hurt. Considering all we've been through together... I thought we were friends..."

Bai looks over to Spring, stitching her eyebrows together.

"I can explain..."

"No need my dear," The spider lady cuts her off. "I really don't have time to deal with sentimental stuff. I already gave my services for the day, so I'm going to just collect my debt."

"What kind of debt?" Bai asks, a slight tremor in her voice.

"I'm sorry Bai. It was the only way... "

"Tell me! What is it?!" Bai insists.

"Ladies, ladies! Cut the drama. I won't lift a finger on either of you... I just want the human." She eyes him hungrily with her black eyes.

"No!" Bai immediately steps in front of him.

"A deal is a deal."

"How could you? You promised him to her when you know how much he means to me!" Bai looks accusingly at Spring. "Take me instead, I'll do whatever you want, just leave him be."

"You're no use to me, snake! I make it my business to take human souls... especially those loved by a spirit such as yourselves. They are the most potent!" She grins as she turns back into a spider and slips past Bai in the blink of an eye. She grips the human with one of her legs and drags him away with her.

"No! Help me!!" His cries are shortly cut off when the spider lady clogs his mouth with silk.

"Ugh, I hate it when they wail…" She bites him on the arm injecting venom as he loses consciousness.

"I won't let you do this!" Bai wails. She transforms into a snake, the first time she has done so willingly in a very long time, and fights the spider. Spring stares at them fighting each other, unable to decide which side to take. The spider tosses her prey aside temporarily, as she deals with her new threat. Bai tries to wrap her body around the spider, but she is slippery and evades her easily.

"Don't hurt her…" Spring manages to say.

"I see why Greenie was so entranced with you… You are a feisty one." The spider lady muses. "Pity…" The spider lady lunges towards her and Bai is unable to evade in time as her teeth sink into her. The spider's venom momentarily paralyzes Bai, but it is enough for the spider lady to recuperate her prey and disappear. Spring comes to her aid, wanting to help her to lift herself up as she transforms back into a human.

Bai refuses her hand and sweeps it aside.

"I'm sorry, I-I know I hurt you, I only did this because I had no other options." Spring says, tears filling her eyes.

"You could have left me there. I would have been fine."

"No, I couldn't," Spring continues to sob.

"I know, I'm selfish. I just wanted you to be free. Now that you are… I think… I- think it's best that I leave… I'm sorry"

"I'm sorry too."

"I won't ever stop loving you Bai, but I know you cannot forgive me."

"No, I guess not." Bai pushes back her tears, looking away. This was the only time when Spring saw Bai almost breaking down.

Spring resists the urge to comfort Bai and hug her as she knows she will be rejected if she tries. She lingers for a moment taking in Bai's sweet aroma before turning around and walking away.

***

BAI PICKS HERSELF UP, faltering as she tries to walk, but she keeps on going, hoping that she can find her lost husband.

Upside Down

By Chantal Finn-Losier

I CLOSE MY EYES. I don't need to look. First, I place my right fingers inside the cuff of the glove on my left hand and pull, holding on to the inside out glove with my protected hand. I insert my bare fingers inside the cuff of the glove on my right hand and peel it off. I complete the dance of the dirty gloves by dunking the wrinkled plastic ball in the waste basket below. *Voilà!* I open my eyes and can't help but smile my satisfaction. Since I have to do this countless times in a day, I might as well have fun with it. To the humans within these walls, routinely handling the patients' blood, urine and feces is a vector for germs, viruses, and bacteria; wearing protective skins on one's hands is part of the rules here. Better safe than sorry. I totally get that.

My shift is done but I'm not in any rush to leave the clinic. I enjoy the surroundings and no one is waiting for me at home. At first, I didn't pay any attention to the clock until it hit me that I was not going to make any friends by working past the time next to my name on the weekly schedule.

Full disclosure, I don't deserve all the credit for cracking the code on this one since Maureen did tell me "Katia, you're not gonna make any friend here by staying past your shift. What are you trying to prove?" which sounded like a question although I knew it wasn't. I don't always get their innuendos, but I did get that one.

I walk to the double grey metal doors and push open the door to the right. Here, the doors have little windows at eye level to check that no one on the other side gets slammed by the door. Shit! I forgot to look. Again! I already know when the path is clear but I don't want to get in trouble with management for not following the rules. Next time, I have to at least bring my face near the glass before pushing. Next time. Michael calls it "to take a mental note" so I'm mentally writing it down. I walk to the lunchroom which is also where employees leave personal belongings.

"Done for the day, Katia?"

"You bet, Janet! Three down, two to go." Janet chuckles. I like knowing my audience. Mind you, some humans are easier to read than others so I'm not letting it go to my head. I stop in front of my locker. 30-18-21. Click. I open the door. My purse and my lunch bag are patiently waiting for me. I grab the purse's handle and swing it over my left shoulder. I repeat for the lunch bag although with caution. I am indifferent to the purse but I care about the lunch bag. I have to say that I never eat lunch with my co-workers. When our schedules coincide, I simply sit at the lunch table with Michael while he eats his food. I enjoy our chats but it never crossed my mind to consume the content of my lunch bag in front of him. I cannot imagine what it could do to our friendship…

I close the locker door and head for the back entrance reserved for employees. I wave the plastic card with my picture on it over the lock pad and watch the little light go from red to green. I push the door open and anticipate the joy of sun rays hitting my face. Even all by myself, I giggle at the irony. Look at me having a sense of humor!

As soon as I step outside, I feel the contrast between the air-conditioned clinic and the humidity of August. At least, the enemy in the sky is safely covered by a merciful blanket of dark grey clouds. If I close my eyes, I can almost feel a soft drizzle on my nose. Ok, I'll admit to the total absence of drizzle, but it is still awesome out here. Perfect weather for a harmless walk home.

I reach the sidewalk and let my mind wander. It was a busy day at work, which translates to a productive one for me. I did not see Michael, however. Our shifts don't always match and for once I am immensely relieved. Our last encounter was awkward to say the least and I need some time to process the situation.

I met Michael on my first day at the clinic. My head was engulfed in my locker when I heard a laugh nearby. Not a belly laugh but more like a deep slow chuckle. "That's a good one." I looked in the direction of the voice and saw a guy wearing a similar version of my uniform leaning on the locker door next to mine. He was smiling and I remember thinking that his eyes were an interesting mix of grey and blue. "Clever." And his chin pointed in the direction of my tattooed upper arm displaying a giant mosquito in full bite. "I'm Michael." He extended his right arm in my direction.

"Katia. With a K."

"I know." He winked at me. "You're the new girl I'm spending the day with."

"Hm?!"

"Look at the schedule." He pointed to a board on the wall. "You're shadowing me today." He flashed me a huge smile before opening his locker. I remember noticing he had perfect teeth.

Michael turned out to be a really good teacher. He made sure I understood every part of the job and was amazing with the patients. With the ladies, he flirted just enough to steal the show from the needle. He talked sports to the guys until they forgot about the stinger. He was surprisingly comfortable with the kids and usually succeeded at making them laugh, even the ones on the brink of tears.

I turn into the driveway to my apartment and reach in my coat pocket for the key. I never even bothered to remove the little tag where Mrs. Alice, the owner of the place, had written 11-B in black marker. The minute I told Mrs. Alice that I was taking the place, she slapped the key on the kitchen counter without ceremony. "It's yours, young lady. You better not be the party type."

It was my first experience apartment-hunting and not one that I am in any rush to repeat. My online searches kept showing disappointing results of lofts with suspicious descriptions such as "bright and airy," "lots of windows," and "high ceiling." I feared it sounded too good to be true when I came across Mrs. Alice's humble offering of a "1 bedroom basement apartment. Furnished. Available now." An additional line for her name and telephone number. I could tell Mrs. Alice was paying by the word for this ad.

I will confess that my expectations were low – I had seen at least a dozen of those offensive places already - but I was extremely pleased with this one. The narrow building was described to me as having "character."

Unit 11 is a two-bedroom apartment on the ground floor, 11-A is also a two-bedroom but on the second floor, and 11-B is a one-bedroom basement apartment. The unit in the basement is smaller because the basement also has a utility room to accommodate the furnace and the hot water tanks. The old couple in 11 have occupied the unit for twenty-three years and are pretty quiet. The two guys living in 11-A are roommates and both work at the local factory. I still had not asked a single question but Mrs. Alice was chatty so I just nodded a lot.

The entryway to 11-B consists of a concrete staircase going down for 8 steps facing a red door. Whoever painted it last, applied a different shade than the previous red. Interestingly, those various coatings were meant to cover a door that was red in the first place. I can tell from the wonderful assortment of peeling paint dislodging itself in multiple tones of red. I guess it would suffice to say that the door is red. And I love my red door! As soon as I laid my eyes on it, I knew I was nowhere near the nonsense of my previous viewings. I could not hide my enthusiasm when Mrs. Alice guided me through a small hallway to the living space. I was all "Ahh…" and "Ohh…" which seemed to confuse Mrs. Alice who stopped her chatter. Seriously, what a gem! First of all, the ceiling was miraculously of normal height. Yes, there was a smallish window above the couch in the living room and a similar one in the bedroom, but nothing there that good drapes could not fix. The rest of the place, well, you know, a fridge and stove, a little table, a bed, the kind of things you usually find in apartments. "I'll take it!" Mrs. Alice raised an eyebrow and sealed the deal with a nod of her tightly curled head.

It hit me that I am daydreaming in front of my beloved red door. I insert the key in the lock and wiggle the handle while pushing with my shoulder as instructed by Mrs. Alice. The red door protests a little but eventually opens up with a squeak. I step inside and stop short in the hallway. I am not alone. And I know that smell. The formidable perfume sends a shiver down my spine. I pause for a moment and call, "Isabella?"

Mocking laughter answers me. Oh, do I remember this sound! I walk to the bedroom and there she is, defiantly sprawled onto *my* bed with a lazy smirk on those pouty red lips of hers. A thick curtain of black eyelashes casts a shadow on her half-closed eyes. "Surprise, sis."

Shutting closed my own eyes does not erase the nightmare unfolding in front of me. Shit. Shit. Shit! Isabella has landed. I turn on my heels and go to the kitchen where I need to lean on the counter for support. I gather that my head is moving from side to side in a futile effort to negate reality. I take a deep breath, exhale slowly and return to the bedroom. "What are you doing here?"

Isabella's sarcastic giggle is torture to my ears. "I'm happy to see you too, Katia! How long has it been? A hundred years?" Literally, yes, and it's way too soon for a reunion. Of course, I do not say it out loud. Like an annoying cat that I do not want on my bed, she yawns and takes her sweet time to stretch her long limbs. She must have been asleep for hours. "Alright. We'll catch up later. I'm outta here. Isabella. Is. Hungry."

Oh, oh! Alarm bells! I can't let her leave. I want her to go but I can't let her. I know how she operates and I don't want it on my conscience or whatever the expression is. How I wish I could wipe that stupid smirk off her stupidly perfect face, for a start! I summon my best authoritative tone. "You're not going anywhere. My roof, my rules." Isabella raises a flawless eyebrow. Thankfully, she seems more amused than offended so I push my luck further. "Come on, girl, let me be a good host and at least feed you." I try to act nonchalant when I let my purse drop to the floor, turn around and walk back to the kitchen carrying the lunch bag with both hands. I metaphorically high-five myself when she follows me to the kitchen.

I am sitting on one chair with the lunch bag in front of me on the table. Isabella approaches and sits on the other side. It was not a big dilemma since I only have two chairs. The table is one of those little round tables with a center metal pillar and four legs at the bottom of the pillar that are popular in coffee shops. Now, it could be the fault of the table, it could be the fault of the floor, maybe they are both guilty, but despite my best efforts, I cannot stop that table from wobbling. There is an entire collection of objects under the legs: pieces of folder paper, paper clips, a lid… nothing does the trick.

I place a hand on the lunch bag. Isabella follows my every move so I take my sweet time to unzip the top part of the bag and flip open the panel. She purses her pretty mouth. Her lips have that eternal shiny crimson tint that makes me wonder if it comes from her last meal. I slowly grab the ice pack and put it on the table. I want to make it longer but there is nothing left for me to do other than reveal the *plat de resistance*. One by one, I pull out the thirteen little vials from the bag and line up the precious flasks between us on the table. Isabella frowns and looks at me. I immediately look down. My newfound aplomb has left me. I am unable to make eye contact. Silence. More silence. I can't take it anymore. "Isabella… I'm… a… a… nurse." I almost choke on the last word.

Back to silence and then Isabella bursts out laughing. "That's why you're wearing pajamas!"

***

THAT NIGHT, I'M WIDE AWAKE ON THE COUCH. Isabella sleeps during the day yet she declares my bedroom as her private quarters for the duration of her stay. I still have no clue why she's here but I should find out soon enough. For now, I am immensely relieved that there was enough in my bag for the two of us. For the tenth time, I look down at my phone. Still nothing. I can't remember the last time Michael and I went an entire day without making contact. I reach for the phone and write him a text. Pause. I don't press send. Instead, I delete every word I just wrote.

***

TODAY, I WENT TO WORK, did my thing and came back to the sofa. I'm off for the next two days so I was forced to take more risks on the job. To collect enough for me and my special guest, I took maximum advantage of my patients who turned their heads away at critical times. I went as far as wearing short sleeves to expose my tattoo as a distracting conversation piece. Desperate times call for desperate measures as the saying goes. As long as Isabella is satisfied, she can go as she pleases, but no one wants to cross paths with a fasting Isabella.

All I want to do now is seek refuge in my private hideout. Shortly after moving in, I discovered the perfect spot to spend my evenings. On this side of the street, all the backyards border onto a wooden area. I found an old bench in the storage shed and dragged it as close to the tree line as the fence let me. Away from the city, the nights are dark and I enjoy sitting here, surrounded by the sounds and creatures of the night.

I'm alone on the bench but my mind is still racing. The familiar flapping of the bats' wings as they rapidly move upward and backward and around this and over that surrounds me but does not bring me its usual comfort. Tonight, their chit-chatting and bickering only reminds me of the time I overheard Martha in the lunchroom telling Karen about her son begging for a bat shelter for his science project. "What the heck are they teaching kids nowadays? A bat house! I *hate* those ugly critters!" The more I rub shoulders with the humans, the more I realize that many prefer to hate what they fear.

Second day without a word from Michael. Today was his second day off before starting the next round of shifts tomorrow. I already knew that so what did I expect? For him to drop by at the start of my break pretending to look for his wallet as he had done so many times before? Or for him to knock on my red door after dinner alleging his TV had just died?

I remember the very first time he came over after work. He looked different even though the smile was the same, and I clued in that he was wearing jeans instead of scrubs. From the doorway, he had handed me a large cardboard box.

"I didn't know what you like so one half is pepperoni and one half is veggies."

He brought pizza. Shit! "Garlic?"

"Garlic? In the sauce, yeah, I imagine."

"It's all yours then. I'm super allergic to garlic." Allergies are so convenient. Mind you, I wouldn't dare to say I am allergic to *all* food. I tried that once and got a huge lecture for apparently making fun of people with eating disorders even though it was absolutely not my intention. Apart from that incident, allergies are definitely my friends. The garlic one is a life savior. And photosensitivity is so useful on sunny days. Premature aging and skin cancer can only go so far but photosensitivity is so much better. That night with Michael, I also had the good sense to drop in the conversation a made-up pet peeve about people going through other people's fridges. "The nerves, right?" It may make me sound weird but certainly not on the same level as him actually opening up my fridge door.

On another one of Michael's regular visits, we were talking about this and that. At some point, he became silent and ran his finger up my upper arm, tracing the contour of my tattoo.

"So? What's the story?"

"I find it fascinating that they feed on blood without hurting."

"Without hurting?! Katia!" His slow laugh sounded accusatory. "Malaria! Yellow fever! West Nile! Zika! Dengue!" He punctuated each new catastrophe with an additional raised finger on his right hand. A fine-looking hand... Masculine... Strong... "Katia? Are you listening?" I remember forgetting about the mosquito bashing.

Today, I spent my entire first day on the couch while Isabella sleeps in my bed. Her presence here is still a mystery. I miss my bedroom but even more importantly I know how to choose my battles so I'm treading lightly. All day, I counted and re-counted the tiles on the ceiling. Anything, really, to stop the memories from high-jacking my brain.

Isabella eventually wakes up and makes her way to the fridge. I join her at the table despite not being hungry at all. I force myself to empty a few vials with her, just for the sake of not raising suspicions.

At sunset, I go for a walk around the block. Upon my return, as soon as I step inside I sense the presence. I walk down the hall slowly, cross my arms behind my back and stop at a safe distance. From the living room, Isabella is beaming. "Katia! Look who's here!" Oh, she's having fun.

***

"HI." MICHAEL SMILES STIFFLY AT ME and looks terribly uncomfortable.

"Hey Michael." On the outside, I'm calm. Inside, I'm freaking out! What on earth did Isabella tell him?!

"Sis, don't stay there. Come sit." She's playing the charm card and pats the empty spot next to her on the sofa.

"Just a minute, I need to go change."

"Change? Why? You look fine." She turns to Michael grinning from ear to ear. "Michael, doesn't she look pretty?" She's enjoying herself way too much. I don't wait for an answer and hurry to the bedroom. I close the door behind me and make a beeline to the closet. I grab the box on the floor and turn it upside down to release its content on the bed. I grab a foam pad, a roll of gauze and adhesive tape and get to work on my forearm. Isabella comes in without knocking. She better not come here to tell me I'm invading her space!

"Katia, he's *yummy*..." I glance at her and see her emerald eyes turn a shade darker.

"Don't you dare!"

"What? I didn't do anything." She looks all innocent which is exactly why I cannot trust her. I clench my jaws. "Isabella..."

"Calm down! He just got here." She looks at my forearm. "Katia, what the hell?" As much as I don't want to, I have to brief her so she doesn't blow my cover.

"I hurt myself at work a few days ago. I shouldn't be healed." My explanation lights up a sparkle in her eyes. My misery is utterly amusing to her.

"The challenges of honest living." She winks and exits the room.

***

I DID HAVE A SILLY ACCIDENT AT WORK LAST WEEK. Silly but not without consequences. There is a gas cooktop in the lunchroom and someone left a burner on. I was caught up in a conversation, leaning on the counter, totally oblivious to the fact that the blue flame had been skimming my forearm. A nasty burn resulted. In a split second, Michael had guided me to the sink where he proceeded to cool the wound. He was in full nurse mode, absorbed by the task, dosing each gesture with equal efficiency and carefulness. We didn't talk. I just watched him apply one of those special foam pads with the moisturizing gel that does not stick to damaged skin and maintain it in place with gauze.

He placed the final piece of adhesive, looked at me and smiled. Whenever he smiles, his eyes narrow a little bit and tiny crinkles appear in the corners. "The bandage has to be changed every…" He stopped mid-sentence, his smile widened and his eyes narrowed some more. "Why am I telling you this? Of course, you know what to do!" Of course, I knew what to do, which was nothing at all. My eyes were locked on his. Michael stopped smiling. "Better?" His voice had a raspy tone to it as if it required effort to speak. Only one word was pronounced but I heard so much more. He was still wearing scrubs but I was no longer his patient. I slowly nodded yes. We were hypnotizing each other. I couldn't say for sure if the tickling I felt was from my damaged skin cells actively healing themselves or for another obscure reason. In slow motion, Michael leaned in and his lips glided on my forehead. I closed my eyes. The tickling grew stronger. In what felt like an eternity, his lips were finally on mine. This was a very dangerous game. I didn't care if a colleague walked in, it sure wouldn't be proper work etiquette but everyone here already assumed we were an item, so… It was dangerous because I had identified the tickling and could not ignore it any longer. I had to leave. And fast!

I pushed Michael out of the way and stormed out of the clinic without even looking back. I had no choice. Every second counted. I rushed home and called my supervisor, pretending to be in too much pain to finish my shift. By then, she had heard of the burner incident and was so empathetic that I felt a little shame. As for Michael, I ignored all his calls and deleted his messages as they came. For that, I felt a lot of shame. I couldn't share all this with Isabella.

Isabella! Shit! I can't leave her alone with Michael. I brace myself and head to the living room.

"Something to drink, Michael?" Since pizza night, I keep beverages in the fridge for when he comes over. It goes without saying that I always bring the can to him myself. It became our inside joke.

"No, thanks." Still no smile. I have never seen him so solemn. It sure doesn't help that Isabella is watching us like a hawk.

"So Michael? Your TV is broken again?" He seems to relax a little bit and gives me a half smile. I'm encouraged. "Wanna go for a walk?" He nods his assent.

We walk in silence for a while. I'm looking for words but am unable to put them together. Michael stops and I do the same. "Katia…" I hear pain in his voice and see sadness in his eyes. And I know too well that I am responsible for both.

"I'm so sorry…" *He's* sorry? I'm confused.

"For what?" His turn to appear puzzled.

"For kissing you at work. I was so out of line." Oh, that's what he thinks.

"Well… we're both guilty on that one." He frowns.

"So… where did I screw up?"

"You didn't. You're not the problem, I am." It's not you, it's me? Did I seriously say *that*? "Michael… I… I…" I really don't know how to get out of this one.

"Is there… someone else?"

"No, no. Nothing like that."

"Katia, whatever it is, just tell me. *Please!*" I look at the ground in silence. "Do you trust me?"

I nod yes.

"Then talk to me." He shakes his head. "Why the secrets? Why didn't you tell me your sister was visiting? Heck, why didn't you tell me you even *have* a sister!" He takes a step back and runs his hand through his hair. He sighs loudly. "I don't get it. I thought we were good together. Please just tell me what's wrong." I understand that he has questions, yet I can't give him answers. He steps forward and takes my right hand in his. "Katia, I like you. A lot." I look at him and I know he means it. Foolishly, I answer by leaning on him and putting my head on his chest. His arms are instantly around me and his head on top of mine. I feel his energy and take a deep breath to fill my lungs with his masculine fragrance. What am I doing?! I know I'm playing with fire and poking the bear inside me but I can't help myself. "Katia, I want nothing more than to be with you, but if that's not what you want, I won't bother you again. Promise. Just tell me where I stand." He takes my face between his hands and I close my eyes, now submerged by the infamous tickling. The roof is on fire and the bear is angry.

I summon all my self-control to remove myself from his embrace. "I'm so sorry, Michael. You don't know how sorry I am." My voice is a whisper. I walk backwards. "Please don't follow me." I turn around and start running in the direction of my apartment. I need to put distance between us, as much distance as possible. Michael doesn't come after me. He won't. I would cry if I just knew how.

I am still running when I reach my driveway. I don't bother going inside and go straight to the bench. Isabella must have been awaiting my return because she's sitting next to me almost immediately.

"Hey! Where's the man-candy?" I shoot her daggers with my eyes and she chuckles. Moments later her attention goes to a bat flying by. "Look Katia! He looks like Uncle Henry!"

"I'm not in the mood." I am *so* not in the mood. The only person I want to be with now is Michael and he is the last person I can approach. Isabella is my sister but... How true it is that we can choose our friends but not our family. And even if I had a friend, I couldn't share this with a friend. I am afraid that the only being I can confess this to is...

"Isabella?" I really hope I will not regret this later. "I screwed up. Big time."

She tilts her head to the side. "You? You screwed up? You?"

Okay, I need to take the plunge. I take a deep breath, turn my head towards her and purse my upper lip. In the moonlight, I don't doubt that my extended enamels are shining, probably just to daunt me.

"WOAH!" She looks impressed. "I didn't know you had it in you. You know, growing up, I wondered if you even knew how." She pauses and puts two and two together. "Oh, oh! The man-candy... Did you...?"

"No. No! But I left right on time."

And I told her the whole story. How it became increasingly dangerous for him to be with me. How the tickling became increasingly overpowering until I had to leave in a rush to hide my morphed canines. How I needed to protect Michael from... well, me. Isabella listened attentively. She didn't make fun of me. I was starting to see a different side to her. Could it be a new and improved version? An Isabella 2.0...

"Katia?"

"Hmm."

"Just go for it!"

"What?"

"Go for it. Turn him!" I guess the original Isabella is back.

"I CANNOT do that!" I am horrified at the thought. Why did I confide in her again? Isabella shrugs.

"Okay. I'll do it for you." What did she just say?! I look at her and am relieved to see she's only making fun of me. "Seriously, why don't you do it? The more the merrier."

"You can't be serious. He deserves a normal life."

"That's overrated!" She's truly exasperating. We sit in silence for a while.

"Katia?"

"Hmm?"

"Do you have... like... feelings for the human?" I ponder on her question for a while.

"I think so."

"Oh, that's big." She appears pensive.

"Katia?"

"Hmm?"

"Is this what the livings call *love*?"

"I guess so."

"How is it?"

"What?"

"*Love*. How is it?"

"Painful."

I could never forgive myself for hurting Michael. All my life, I worked so hard to do things differently. Isolating myself from my kind only resulted in me royally screwing up on my own.

"Isabella, why are you here?" I still have no idea.

"Well… You're not the only one who messed up and I needed a break from the gang." Oops, I'm not pulling on that tread. "You know, I never looked up to you when we were like… much younger."

"Thanks?" I wonder where she is going with this.

"You always refused our lifestyle and I guess I was curious to see how things worked out for you."

"Me, the outcast, and you, the *traditional* one. Isabella: the pride of the family."

"That too, is overrated." She winks at me.

We spend the night on the bench, catching up and basically getting to know each other again. She tells me she is planning on leaving tonight and wants me to join her.

Today is my second day off, and also my second day spent on the couch counting the ceiling tiles. I'm due back at work tomorrow but I cannot risk a rapprochement. Knowing Michael has opened me up to a range of emotions that I did not even know existed. I failed miserably at protecting the one who became the most important to me. My fangs never touched him yet I somehow punctured his soul.

***

AT SUNSET, I DRAG MY FEET TO THE BENCH where the nightlife is already in full swing. Sitting in the dark, I realize that I miss flying. If I had said something like that at work, Martha would go on and on about her plane phobia and I wouldn't bother to clarify that sitting in a plane is not flying. I never boarded a flight and have no desire to do so. What I miss is *flying*.

The night is enticing. The darkness, a friendly presence. My senses are on full alert. I am completely aware of my surroundings yet unable to locate the answer. I am all ears but cannot hear any solution. Seeing the world from upside down does not let me see a way out. I can't stop thinking about Michael yet I have no answer, no solution, no way out. Maybe one day things will be different for us but for now, I need to keep him safe. Other bats are zipping around in the dark. It feels good to spread my wings. I release my grip and follow the echo. Flying is liberating. I close my eyes. I don't need to look.

Rachel's Keeper

SL Deslippe

"YOU CAN ALWAYS TELL A PATTERMAN BY THE SHAPE OF HIS thumb." So my father would boast to all who would listen but not without cause. While some of us had black hair or white hair or no hair at all, we all shared the same queer trait of an inordinately long thumb on our left hand. From my great-great-great-grandfather Patterman, who's overlong thumb piloted a ship full of the earliest settlers to Sumer, to his son, who built a church on arrival that stands to this day as a testament to the skills of long-thumbed labourers. My father even swore that the slanted, irregular script on the earliest colony marriage records suggest that the notary who maintained it wrote with an uneven left hand. Indeed, it seemed that every corner of

Sumer was in some way a tribute to my family legacy that it's no wonder that my father took pride in our name, our history, and our Patterman thumbs.

He married my mother – she too, a long-thumbed Patterman – when she came of age. He idolized her but any affection she had for him was overtaken by anger stemming from grief. My older brother Adam never lived to see his first birthday and I don't know that my mother ever forgave my father for his death. In time she gave birth to me and to the shock of all who saw my purple, misshapen form writhing in the cradle, I lived – a privilege my father attributed to my lucky inheritance of the Patterman thumb. But while my father was relieved to have a son to protect the family legacy, my presence only seemed to add to my mother's melancholy. If truth be told, I don't think she ever truly saw me as a son, rather a living reminder of a son she no longer had.

Her health continued to decline and in the end, it was Rachel who absorbed what remained of her strength, and she died giving Rachel life. We feared Rachel would follow but my father refused to hear it. He used up all that was left in him to ensure her recovery before following my mother, leaving Rachel and I alone. In hindsight I think this was my first exposure to the possibility that life is finite. Of course I recognize that human beings are mortal and no life can be sustained indefinitely. What I realized is that maybe civilization can only sustain a fixed amount of life-energy, and we spend our lives looking for accessible reserves that we can leech off of unsuspecting hosts to prolong our existence. If this is true, only two means of survival truly are available to us. The first and most obvious is to maintain a positive sum of life-energy relative to your peers. The second is imparting a legacy that supersedes that of those around you and retains influence long after your life-energy drains away.

Of course, legacies don't come cheap. As the last surviving male from a once proud, established family, I know this better than most. With each generation, the minimum threshold for 'legacy' is pushed a little higher so that any man intending to climb over it must stand shoulder-to-shoulder with the gods. There is no longer a need for innovation; the time for piloting ships and building churches has long since passed. What Sumer needs now is a Keeper. Someone who recognizes the importance of all that came before him and does his utmost to ensure that they are not lost to time.

***

"…THE YIELDS ARE LESS THAN HALF OF LAST YEAR'S and aren't fit to feed the pigs. My most optimistic estimates suggest that we might be able to cover the interest owed but only if the blight passes before the fall harvest."

The room fell silent. No one dared lift his head and lock eyes with his brother. We knew in our hearts that the yield was poor but conceding this felt like a public admission of failure.

Finally Mr. Jacobs, the town magistrate spoke.

"And the principal?" he asked.

"Impossible," Mr. Clemmons, the notary answered. "The silos are barren, but for mold and beetles. Even if the fall harvest proceeds as hoped we could not possibly generate the means to pay down our debt."

"You must appeal for more time," Doctor Machen interjected. "The village is starving. Men are dying in the fields for want of a decent meal. Surely even the most calloused creditor will take pity on a community struck by a blight of beetles. How could we have foreseen this?"

"The argument is not that we should have foreseen it but that we should have prepared for the possibility," Mr. Clemmons answered. "The creditors impressed upon me last year that their patience was waning and they would not tolerate further tardiness."

The room once again lapsed into silence. Finally, Mr. Jacobs cleared his throat and began to speak.

"In the early days of our settlement, before the fields and livestock had matured, we trapped animals off the land. Their meat is passable and the fur will generate greater earnings than we could have made off the fields."

Samuel looked up and shook his head. "That would require us to go into the forest."

"What of it?" Mr. Jacobs answered.

Samuel looked apprehensive. He glanced nervously around the room, seeking support but when none was forthcoming, he spoke.

"There are Others," he whispered.

Mr. Jacobs frowned before responding. "That's impossible," he began, "the nearest village is three days journey from here."

Here I spoke. "I can tell you with complete certainty that Others exist, and whatever they are, they did not come from any village of ours." All eyes in the room looked to me. Some appeared curious, others fearful, but it was the disbelieving expressions of the very men appointed to lead us that inspired me to continue.

"A year ago, I never would have believed it possible. At first, I assumed I was imagining it. A trick of the light, or a light breeze perhaps. In all recorded history we never found a scrap of evidence suggesting there were other inhabitants anywhere near Sumer. It wasn't until the blight began that the Others appeared, like a tide creeping in off the sea, bringing death and desertification in their wake."

"But what are they?" Mr. Clemmons asked.

"I couldn't say," I answered. "Shadows mostly. I've never been close enough to know for sure. But the other night I awoke and saw one of them at my window. Tall, thin, angular, and unnaturally fast. It scattered at the sound of my voice but not before I garnered a good look at its eyes. Hollow, and black as beetles."

"But you'd just woken up," Doctor Menchen countered. "Is it possible you were dreaming? Or you imagined it?"

"I know the difference between dreams and reality, and I know what I saw," I growled, my brows furrowed, and my hands clenched into fists out of sight.

"It's true," Samuel began. "I've seen them too. Never up close though. It's like you said." He turned to me, either to offer assistance or demand it, I could never be sure which. "They hide in shadows and return to them just as soon as they come. It's like they are shadows, but a shadow don't eat."

"Eat?" Mr. Clemmons asked.

I shrugged. "You said yourself sir, the silos are barren."

"From the blight!" Mr. Jacobs yelled impatiently. "Anything they contained was thrown away because it was infested with-"

"Beetles," I added.

"Are you suggesting that something unnatural is at play?" Mr. Jacobs demanded.

"I am merely identifying correlation," I answered. "I leave the rest to you to draw your own conclusions. But I implore you to consider the possibility that the Others and the blight may be linked."

The room once again fell silent as the assembly contemplated the significance of my charge and how to proceed.

"Is there a place or a time when they tend to conger?" Mr. Clemmons asked gently.

"Usually at night," I answered. "I couldn't say what becomes of them during the day, but we suspect they retreat into the forest. As for where, we're still unsure but it would have to be dark and sheltered as they seem to fear the light. As Samuel says, we never get close enough to ascertain their purpose and the few times we've seen them have been by surprise."

"Is anyone keeping track of the sightings?" he asked. "This might help us determine what they are and why they're here."

"No, though I suppose that would be wise," I conceded.

"Indeed it would," Mr. Jacobs interjected. "Based on your description any one of us could be the culprits. All you've told us of these creatures is they have shadows and their eyes are coloured black."

I felt my anger boiling to the surface again. "Of course, black isn't a colour though, right sir?" I began testily.

"I'm sorry?"

"Black is uncoloured. Shine a light through a prism and all the colours will eventually converge as white. White is Every Thing. Black, on the other hand, is No Thing. I always found that interesting. That a thing could be defined entirely by what it isn't."

The meeting was adjourned shortly thereafter and I quickly made my way from the hall, as did many of the other farmers at the table. Ordinarily we might have accompanied each other on the walk home but after being ridiculed for our knowledge of the Others, I think we all felt that we'd said our piece.

"The problem with leaders," my father told me, *"is they look too hard at where they're going that they forget where they are. An intelligent man may believe that*

he can find his way across the ocean armed with nothing but a compass and his wits. A wise man knows that he won't make it out of the harbour unless he can learn to read the waves. Nature can be angry, vindictive and cruel. That's why a compass will never be more than a means of expediting ignorant geniuses towards their own demise. Never use a compass. Follow your North Star if you will but never take your eyes off the waves."

When I returned home, I was surprised to see the lights extinguished. The hour was late, but I'd never known Rachel to go to bed before I got home. She'd not been well of late, but I just attributed this to the same malnourishment from which the whole village was suffering. She still prepared meals and kept the house, albeit a bit slower than she had before the blight. Perhaps her strength was failing?

I quickened my step. As soon as I got home, I made my way directly to Rachel's room, where I was further surprised to find the door ajar. I pushed it open and glanced eagerly around the room for any sign of strife.

There was none. The room was arranged exactly as I'd left it. The bed was made, the furniture upright, the clothes neatly arranged in the dresser drawers, the only difference was the complete absence of any sign of Rachel.

I felt a sudden chill and realized that the window was slightly ajar. I slowly made my way towards it and rested my hands on the sill as I looked outside for any sign of her. I stayed there for some time before a sharp, searing pain in my left hand brought me back to the present.

I looked down and saw to my shock and disgust that my hands were covered in beetles.

***

"YOU HAVE MY SYMPATHY, BUT UNDER THE CIRCUMSTANCES I'm afraid it's not possible. The men are exhausted from long hours with barely any food or water. There is absolutely no one to be spared for a search."

I felt my insides writhe in anger but when I spoke it was with a voice of determined calm.

"I can assure you Mr. Jacobs that I am well aware of our situation," I began. "But a crime of this magnitude cannot go unacknowledged."

"How can you be so certain there was a crime?" he responded curtly. "By your own admission, there was no sign of any disturbance or foul play, only-"

"Beetles!" I screamed.

"Yes, beetles," Mr. Jacobs responded. "Rachel was never a strong girl, but I trust she had the power to resist being overtaken by a few beetles."

"With all due respect sir, 'a few beetles' have crippled this village with disease and starvation such as we've never seen. More to the point, we've already discussed the possibility that something more sinister than beetles is at play."

"I'm aware of your suspicions but I refuse to further indulge any more superstitious nonsense about other-worldly beetles or shadows that eat."

"There have been sightings!"

"Circumstantial. As of this moment neither you, nor Samuel nor any of the other labourers have produced any hard evidence supporting your claims."

"This is astounding. I've known you to cite a bountiful harvest as an act of providence but when presented with evidence of opposing forces, you refuse to entertain the possibility that evil is abound."

Here his eyes narrowed. "Believe me, I know evil better than most. I witnessed pure, undiluted evil twenty-five years ago when I first locked eyes with your father, and it lingers with me still."

I smiled grimly in response. "Yet you never obtained a confession," I began. "How that must torture you. With all your knowledge and experience and empty threats, you couldn't break him. He never diverged from his story. How do you reconcile your perceived failure with your role as the hand of God? Perhaps God has abandoned you, and evil took his place."

"Enough," Mr. Jacobs responded steely. "Never, throughout my career as magistrate have I ever questioned the presence of God. I believed then as I do now that should the hand of God fail, the will of God would persevere through other means. Even if it took twenty-five years, even if the sins of the father were ultimately absolved by the children, divine restitution was forthcoming and balance would be restored."

"Oh, I hope they take yours next," I growled. Ordinarily I would never have dreamed of reproaching a magistrate in such a manner but watching his smug, condescending expression give way to fear only emboldened me. "When you walk home and find your home as cold and barren as a tomb, with nothing but beetles and unanswered questions for company, you'll know they came for yours. At that moment you'll realize that any lofty ideals you held about divine restitution were powerless to protect the ones you loved. When that happens, you'll know that I'm at peace."

I reached for my satchel filled with whatever meagre supplies I could muster before addressing the magistrate once more. "Your position, while regrettable, is expected. If no men can be spared for a search party, I'll go alone. I'll return with Rachel or as God is my witness, I won't come back at all."

I turned away and set forth into the forest.

***

HOURS TURNED TO DAYS, AND DAYS TO WEEKS, until so much time had passed that I stopped bothering to count. The days grew colder and shorter and I recognized that if I didn't find Rachel before winter began that it was unlikely I'd find her at all. My provisions had long since run out and I'd had little choice but to subsist on fish and wild mushrooms, but even they were likely to disappear once the land froze over. Even as I acknowledged this, pride and a sense of duty to all the Pattermans who came before me kept me from returning to Sumer.

"Think of legacy like a plant," my father told me. *"Plants provide nourishment, but what provides a plant? The sun, the earth, the rain, all operating in tandem to nurture the plant and protect it from harm. We don't often recognize their worth, instead we focus on the plant because that is what we see. But if the elements are corrupted, so too is the plant. That's why focusing on the plant itself is a mistake. Your goal is to foster the elements that produce something worthy of consumption. Good plants will come, but only if the elements are strong. Fail to keep the elements and your plants will die."*

Eventually I found a cave which provided some shelter and no shortage of rats and other vermin, which after months of fish and mushrooms felt like a meal fit for a king. It was on my third night here as I was licking what little meat I could salvage from the bones of a field mouse that I was startled by a piercing shriek reverberating off the cave walls. Startled, I fell back and reached for my satchel. I fumbled inside for my knife while silently reflecting on the futility of such a gesture. How does one stab a shadow?

"But a shadow don't eat," I reminded myself. Emboldened, I unsheathed my knife and prepared for an attack.

The wailing softened as the creature approached. It appeared to be about the size of a human but misshapen. It was large and bulky on one side and lean and shapely on the other. It had legs but no arms, head but no neck, and a low, soothing whisper interspersed with wails. It drew closer, finally stepping into the light of my fire. It was here that my resolve failed me. I dropped my knife in shock and retreated against the cave walls.

"Rachel?"

Rachel looked at me in response before glancing back at the burden she carried. She pulled back the many layers of fabric covering her arms to unveil an infant with beetle-black eyes and an overlong thumb.

"I named him for our father," she said.

***

"WHERE IS HE?" I DEMANDED.

"Calm down," Rachel began. "He's still out hunting and not likely to return until tomorrow. The beetles destroyed most of their reserves and now that the harvest has passed, they have to travel farther for food."

"How many of them are there?"

"Does it matter?" Rachel answered. "Enough to form a village of our own. Some made their way closer to Sumer in search of food, but most remain here in the forest."

"Why didn't you tell me?"

Rachel looked down guiltily before locking eyes with me once more. "I planned to tell you eventually," she began. "It happened so quickly. I was growing bigger by the day and I knew in a few more months I'd be unable to hide it."

"All the more reason for you to tell me! I could ha-"

"I was never yours to touch," Rachel answered coldly. "You were so angry. I'd hoped your anger would cool in time, but you grew more savage every day. I didn't know what to do so eventually he convinced me to leave with him."

"You speak with him?"

"I learned." She turned towards the creature, which had finally ceased wailing and fell asleep on the ground at her side. "I planned to come back and tell you in the spring once the baby grew strong enough to be left alone. I didn't expect you to understand or forgive me, but I wanted to explain everything before I said goodbye."

"You can't seriously be planning on staying?"

"This is my home now," Rachel answered. "It's not one I planned for myself but it's more fulfilling than I ever would have thought possible."

"And what of our life in Sumer?"

"Sumer is dying," Rachel answered simply. "Do you know why the crops are failing? Why the beetles came? It was us. Sumer is desperately trying to impose outdated conventions and systems on a land that cannot sustain them indefinitely."

"Nonsense."

"It's true!" The creature stirred in response to its mothers' voice. Once more, Rachel emitted the low, soothing whisper I'd heard earlier to placate it. "It's true," she repeated. "The only creatures that can thrive under these conditions are beetles. If you can't adapt the entire village will die."

Here an idea took hold in me. "Very well," I began. "What if we all returned to Sumer together? He can explain to the other villagers how to effectively survive here and you can translate for him."

Rachel looked worried. "What if they hurt him," she asked, "or the baby?"

"I'll explain everything when we arrive and your family will be under my protection," I answered. "Just this once. Afterwards you can return to your life here with my blessing."

Rachel continued to look worried. "I'll need to discuss it with him first," she answered.

"Of course," I replied. "Get some rest, and we can all discuss it in the morning."

Rachel smiled and lowered herself by the creature. "Won't you rest as well?" she asked.

"Later," I answered. "I'll wait until the fire goes down."

I stared intently at Rachel until I was certain she was asleep. Afterwards, I silently made my way over to where the creature lay sleeping and flexed my Patterman thumb. Does a shadow feel pain? If a shadow don't eat or breathe or fuck or conceive a child, when exactly does a shadow become a man? What is it my father saw when he stared down at Adam and prepared to assert his birthright by force - man or shadow? Strange isn't it, that a shadow masquerading as a Patterman would meet the same fate as a Patterman who couldn't be a man. Makes you wonder how many other families were broken over the subtle distinction between men and shadows when the difference is only a thumbs-width apart. But gaps create space where doubt can flourish because truth is No Thing. It's defined entirely by the absence of a lie. That's why there will always be Keepers. They keep the shadows of doubt from eclipsing the legacies of pilots and builders, and no hollow threats of divine restitution will convince us to betray them.

My father was right, it was easier than I'd anticipated. Turns out, a shadow don't wail when its time is nigh.

***

I LEFT THE CAVE BEFORE SUNRISE THE NEXT DAY, ostensibly to look for mushrooms but in reality so not to face her when she woke. *She has no grounds to link it to me,* I reasoned. *Tragedies happen. Besides, it looked a sickly little thing from what I saw and there's no telling how much damage a cool night air can inflict on a frail body.* I stayed hidden but close enough to the mouth of the cave that I would hear her scream. I remained there as the morning sun crept higher over the horizon and it was then that I began to worry. It's unreasonable to assume that a young mother would have slept that late. Perhaps she grew suspicious and tried to flee? So I would not take her back with me to Sumer? Finally I decided that enough time had passed that I had no choice but to see what had become of her.

I waited too long. When I re-entered the cave I saw what remained of her draped over the creature, her arms dripping with blood and my knife at her side.

I wish I could tell you that I felt some kind of sorrow but the truth is I didn't feel anything at all. So much of my life's purpose was wrapped up in playing the part of Rachel's Keeper that I couldn't immediately process who I was once that purpose shifted. Eventually I remembered that the role of a Keeper was not necessarily to protect people. Only truths. Just as Adam became legend under my father's watch, so too could Rachel undermine.

I placed what remained of the creature in the fire pit and set it aflame. Afterwards I placed my knife over Rachel's body and waited for him to return.

I suppose the end was inevitable. A legacy of writhing children and overlong thumbs is too great a burden for one man to carry alone indefinitely. Time to bequeath my dagger to An Other so that he might end my suffering and take up the burden alone. I'm confident he'll oblige. And then another me after me for good measure. And then another and another, purportedly to protect what remains of his people but in actuality just to bury his wife and child under a sea of corpses so he can no longer hear them scream. After all, no one ever bothered to learn what became of MacDuff after Dunisane but as one who's spent the better part of his life nursing ghosts, I can tell you that their hunger is insatiable and they don't take kindly to being denied. He'll never stop until the inevitable confrontation with a Keeper, avenging a Rachel of his own.

It's odd; so much effort went in to keeping Rachel safe as if multiplication was the only strategy for preserving our line. We forgot that absorbing life-energy can only delay death while legacies hold the key to immortality. What better legacy could a man ask for than first blood in the final confrontation between man and shadow? As I thought on this a smile crossed my lips and for the first time in my life, I felt confident in my own sense of self-worth. Twenty years ago, no one would have believed that the spindly, writhing gargoyle in the Patterman cradle would amount to anything but never underestimate the strength and determination of overlong thumbs. Even the crudest of our line can inspire lesser thumbs to take up the burden and squash out every last beetle they can find.

Into the Shadows

By Holly LeBlanc

TALA STOOD NEAR THE WALL WITH HER ROOMMATE KATE AND A small group of homogeneous freshmen, trying but failing to feign interest in the painful small talk that was supposed to help lonely souls find one another in this god forsaken place. Young birds with fresh new feathers, leaping with blind faith, or stupidity, or ingrained instinct, into a new life. She smiled slightly at the image, which the overgrown boy with the button-up shirt next to her must have taken as an invitation.

He moved slightly closer. "So, where are you from?"

"London," she said. She looked into her solo cup, wondering if it was empty enough that she could excuse herself for a refill.

"I'm from here, well, pretty close to here," the man-boy offered. "So if you ever need someone to show you around…"

She almost laughed out loud. The campus at Exeter was about the size of a postage stamp. But instead she smiled kindly at him, "Thanks, I'll keep that in mind."

"I honestly don't know why anyone would come here from the big city…" His eyes protruded slightly.

"Sometimes people just have to get away… I guess." She held up her sort-of empty cup, in the universal sign of escape, then wove her way through warm bodies to the kitchen.

It was true, she did come here to get away, but also because she felt a pull to come west. To search out the mysterious link to her mother; something her father had let slip long ago in one of his tirades, before the subject had become completely taboo. Just the name of a place, Umbreton. He had only mentioned once, but she had held it in her memory like a precious jewel. The place where her mother… was from? Ran away to? Left her daughter for?

She closed her eyes and took a deep breath. This was not the time or place to get lost in those questions again.

Returning with a fresh cup of beer (not too full, in case she needed to escape again), she saw that Karen and bug-eyes with a couple of his friends were gathering around a table.

"We're going to play poker!" Karen said. "You in?"

Tala glanced over her shoulder. Where else was she going to go?

Bug-eyes, whose real name was actually Ryan, had two friends that looked pretty old for freshmen. They were large in a healthy, farm-lad sort of way, and both had reddish hair.

"This is Drew, and that's Sammy. They're brothers," Ryan said.

"And exactly how old are you two?" The words slipped out before she could stop them.

Drew looked surprised. "Well, we don't actually go here. We just like the parties." He passed a glance towards Sammy and did something weird with his eyebrows.

As they played poker, a game Tala was quite adept at, she could see that Karen was becoming more confused. And drunk. The two brothers were getting on Tala's nerves. They seemed like blundering fools, but had somehow amassed a significant lead. They had agreed to pay in twenty-five pounds each, and Tala wanted to see it through, but she also thought she should get her roomie out of there.

That's when it happened.

Tala and Karen heard a commotion on the other side of the room and glanced over, but out of the corner of her eye, Tala saw a shadow of a movement. She turned back quickly, and saw Sammy pulling some of Karen's poker chips over the edge of the table and into his hand.

He only had a moment to see Tala's face, a contorted grimace of red anger, before she landed on him, arms flailing. Karen jumped back and out of her chair in a fluid motion, but too late, as Tala sent her beer and poker chips flying onto her dress. Which she didn't even notice.

Tala landed a left hook on Sammy's unprepared jaw, with her full body weight behind it, knocking him off his chair, the back of his head bouncing off the wall then onto the floor. Now on top of him, she continued to pummel his head, knocking it back and forth, all while screaming "You son-of-a-bitch! Bag of slime! Thief! How dare you..." The words became unintelligible, yet louder as the other party-goers hushed and turned to stare.

Finally her punches slowed as Sammy's head and neck went limp. Tala glanced towards Karen, who had turned pale, her back pushed up against the wall for support. Tala wiped the back of her hand on her mouth, then looked aghast at the blood smeared on her own knuckles.

Then back at her victim... there was blood trickling from his nose and the corner of his mouth. He was breathing shallowly, but definitely wasn't awake.

What had she done?

She looked the other way, desperately searching for the exit, when her eyes latched onto a shadow. Between and behind the still forms of shocked freshmen was something else, a dark face shadowed in grey, that was there but not there, eyes glowing red as they bore into Tala.

She stood up slowly, eyes locked on the face, horror and panic rising in her blood. Somehow she knew, this shadowed face was here for her, and whatever had just come over her... whatever had made her into a violent monster, this face had something to do with it.

And it wanted her.

Pushing through the stunned crowd at the back of the room, she found the back door, slammed through it, and ran.

***

SHE DIDN'T STOP UNTIL SHE WAS BACK IN HER DORM ROOM. Door locked, back against the wall and arched as she remembered to breathe again. Deep breaths, bringing herself back. Her arms and legs shaking, she stayed propped against the wall.

What had happened back there? Where had her anger come from? Like a volcano, an unstoppable red force. She watched herself in horror as if she was just an unfortunate witness in the crowd hitting the unconscious asshole, again and again. But she wasn't a witness... she was a brute, a monster... It was too much to process.

And that face. She could see the red glowing eyes, burning right through her own eyes, reading her mind, her soul. Where was it now? What did it want with her? Was it coming for her now that she was here, alone?

In two leaps, she grabbed her duffel bag from the closet, stuffing in her few belongings and grabbing her wallet. Her life in one bag.

She was terrified, but knew she couldn't stay here. Not after what she had done. She needed for it not to have happened. No, she needed to stop it from ever happening again. And she knew it couldn't be a coincidence that the shadowy face had appeared at the exact moment she had lost control. Whoever or whatever was behind those glowing eyes, she needed to find out and stop him, stop *it* from ever coming near her again.

She called a cab to meet her at the end of the street, hoping to avoid Karen or any other party-goers. At least she knew where she was headed. The whole reason she had come to school in Exeter. The only place her father had ever mentioned that could possibly, hopefully help her learn about her mother... and herself.

Umbreton.

***

THE MIDNIGHT TRAIN WAS NEARLY EMPTY, and Tala gratefully settled into her seat, cradling her bag next to her. She gazed out into the darkness, allowing herself a moment with her disbelief. This could not be happening.

Yet it was.

She closed her eyes and immediately realized she was utterly exhausted. She allowed herself to fall away into the dark oblivion of her mind, falling away from the unworldly events of the past few hours.

Then, in her half-conscious mind she saw the two redheads from the poker game, but they were different somehow, older. And there was her father, arguing over the deal, throwing his chips angrily across the table, taking a small flat bottle out of his inside pocket and guzzling it, before glancing in her direction.

And suddenly she was a little girl.

"Shouldn't you be in bed?" he tried to smile away his shame, lurching towards her, his rancid breath washing over her face as he tried to hustle her back up the stairs.

But before she turned to the staircase, she saw. In the dark corner, out of the lamplight, pale at first then glowing brighter. Burning eyes. . In a shadowed face. Her heart beat faster. And this time a long arm emerging from a cloak, with a pale hand, gesturing to... what?

In the dark corner there was somebody else. The face wanted her to see. She struggled against her drunken father. He grabbed her and lifted her precariously into his arms.

"Where d'you think yer going," he slurred.

She looked over his shoulder down into the corner, and saw, surrounded by grey shadow, a young cloaked woman holding a sleeping child. They seemed to be floating slightly above the ground, supported by the greyness.

"Look up," she thought through the dream, but she didn't have a voice. "Look at me."

But the woman didn't move, and the menacing face above her stepped forward, obliterating her from view, the red eyes coming closer, boring in through Tala's eyes.

She screamed.

***

STARTLED AWAKE, SHE WONDERED if she had screamed out loud. She looked down the train car, and only saw two other huddled forms, likely asleep. She looked out the window into utter blackness, the terror of her dream lingering like an old memory. Which it was... sort of. The lights from the train illuminated a couple of feet of wispy grass, and at times Tala could make out wire or wood fencing, but nothing else, and looking up, no stars. Like she was nowhere. She gulped. Umbreton.

Taking out her phone, she checked.

Umbreton. Population 800. Ok.

Hotel: Umberton Inn. No picture, no information, no phone number or website. She really should have thought this through. But at least she would be far away from that face, whoever it was, and whatever it wanted. She shuddered.

"Next stop is yours, miss," the elderly conductor appeared out of nowhere, startling her. "Sorry, miss."

"Do you know where the hotel is?' Tala asked. She suddenly craved human interaction in this darkness, and her heart was once again thumping. What was she doing walking into a strange village in the middle of the night?

"Oh, I've never been meself, but I've come by'ere lots." He had a kind tone, seeming to sense her nervousness. "There's a wee inn right across from the station, on that side." He pointed out her window. Just as he did, yellow street lights came alongside them. Tala felt unaccountably relieved.

"Ye know where you're going? There's strange talk about these parts..." the old man cautioned.

"What?" She could hear the fear in her own voice, and looked down quickly, pretending to gather her things as the train stopped.

"Oh, nothin', really... Sorry I mentioned it." He smiled, trying to reassure her but falling somewhat short. "Just make sure to get across to th' inn. It's late."

She glanced at her phone. Nearly 3 a.m.

"Thank you." She made her way down the aisle and out into the cool dark night.

The train pulled away, leaving the station deserted. The platform was bordered on both sides by cobblestones, which continued into the street. Shriveled petunias bowed their heads in large barrel planters, lit by old-fashioned iron lanterns. The inn was in a row of ancient-looking hunched Tudor-style buildings across the cobbled street. All was silent.

Before crossing, Tala glanced behind her. A yellow street light illuminated two large grey granite pillars with a rusted iron sign between them: "Umbreton Cemetery". Tala could vaguely make out shadowy silhouettes of tilted gravestones and statues through the still darkness. A graveyard... what next? She started to turn to walk across to the inn.

Then suddenly, a tiny light appeared. And another, floating slowly towards her. She froze, catching her breath, just for a moment, then flew across the street. Unbelievably, the doorknob of the inn wouldn't turn, so she grabbed the brass knocker and pounded it as hard as she could, sending booming echoes down the empty street. Breathing hard, she looked over her shoulder, not knowing what to expect.

More lights. Half a dozen, maybe more... meandering closer, up to the edge of the graveyard!

She turned back to the door, heart pumping, hands sweaty as she grabbed for the knocker again.

Instead she stumbled inwards, raised arms landing squarely on the shoulders of a startled teenager. He caught her arms and pushed her upright. "Beg your pardon, ma'am."

"Oh, I-I'm so sorry." She looked over her shoulder at the lights breathlessly, then stepped in... pushing the boy firmly aside, and shut the door, bolting the lock.

"Everything ok, ma'am?' he stepped to the window, looking across the road curiously. "I see you've met our very scary fireflies."

Fireflies?

She looked out the window and saw one of the lights blink off, then a little ways down, it came on again. She gulped, and looked at the teenager, a repressed grin lighting up his eyes.

How embarrassing.

"I- uh. Need a room. Please."

"Aye, you didn't look like you were just dropping by for a visit." Smiling, he turned on a banker's lamp, and pushed through a swinging gate to a small office. The green light shadowed his face ghoulishly as he glanced over a notepad. He looked up, his eyes dark in the gloom, his hair thick and unkempt, but his face... it seemed oddly familiar.

Peering over his shoulder, Tala noticed a small cot, the blankets pulled down. "Were you just sleeping there?"

"Aye. Not many late visitors in the off-season here. Me uncle has me stay down here just in case. It's not so bad really, I get paid just for sleeping mostly."

"Well, sorry for waking you so... suddenly." She glanced downward sheepishly.

"Ah, it's my job. And you're not the only one who's been spooked by our friendly spirits. Could I just take down your name?"

"Tala Woodward."

"Woodward?" he repeated, quickly looking up at her. She thought he blanched a little.

"Yes." She wanted to ask about his reaction, but something stopped her.

He glanced down at his notepad then came around through the gate. "Down the hall this way, Miss Woodward. May I take your bag?"

"No, I've got it. "

She followed him down a narrow, dark-paneled hallway.

"Here we are, and here's your key. If you need anything, you know where to find me. The name's Ben."

"Thank you, Ben." She looked into his face, that strange sense of familiarity again.

She turned the key, and watched as he walked back to his little office. Tomorrow. She would try to find out more tomorrow. For now... she entered the small but tidy room and threw herself on the bed. Darkness and sleep.

***

THE SUN WAS RIDING HIGH ON LAYERED WAVES of clouds when she awoke. It took her a moment to remember where she was: Umbreton. What was she getting herself into, and what was she doing here? Then she thought back to the night before, the bloody fight at the poker game, and shame flooded through her. What kind of person attacked a perfect stranger, albeit one who was robbing her unsuspecting friend? Even so, she could still smell his blood on her hands and feel the stares of the party-goers, and poor Karen, pale and frozen against the wall.

Who was she? Honestly, she didn't even know she could fight like that, and had never so much as punched another person before.

And the face with the red eyes. A shiver ran through her, but she got to her feet, choosing to ignore it. The same face that was in her dreams. Maybe she was just trying to process too much. She splashed water on her face and threw on her hoodie, making her way down the hall.

"Ah! She lives!" The young hotel boy from the night before was sitting behind the desk, grinning.

"Ben," she greeted, remembering his name.

"What can I do for ye?"

"Ben... you seem kind of familiar? Have we met before?"

He smiled, "Not unless ye've been 'ere before. I haven't left this place. Ever. I mean this town, Umbreton. They let me out of the hotel occasionally."

"Well..." She tried to think of a way to explain what she was looking for, but decided to take care of her immediate needs. "Anywhere to eat around here?"

The deli was at the end of the same street, which was only four blocks long. She ordered a sandwich and took it to the train station platform, where she found a bench and ate facing the graveyard. The sun was now surrounded by thick clouds that cast a gloom over everything. The gravestones did seem crooked even in the light of day, as if the inhabitants were shifting uncomfortably in their resting places. Still, it looked way less creepy in daylight, and without fireflies.

She brushed the crumbs off her jeans, then crossed under the iron sign. Her mother came here, she thought. There may be a family connection... but she didn't even have a last name to go on. Still, the place was oddly peaceful when you got past the creepiness of it, and a little exploring might help settle her. Even as this thought crossed her mind, the sun slipped behind a huge swell of clouds, casting deep grey shadows across the gravestones.

She meandered slowly through the graves, many of the first stones too old and pitted for her to read any of their inscriptions. The only words the dead could be remembered by, now also erased by rain and time. Stories and lives, passing forever from memory. Maybe that's why people saw ghosts... because they, too, wanted to be remembered, could not imagine the world without themselves. And so they saw these lingering shades, these fragments of life longing for human connection, reaching out from death...

Tala shivered and pulled her arms across her stomach, moving through the long grass between the rows towards a large stone crypt. She wondered if her mother had walked in this very spot when she had come back here. And if she had been happy to come home... if it indeed had been her home.

A crow cawed and fluttered loudly from a gravestone, disturbing the gloomy peace, and Tala looked up suddenly.

There it was, the face with glowing eyes, crouched beside a tall statue.

She froze, goosebumps up her spine. Was it real?

Then it stood to full height, came around and started walking quickly towards her, closing the space between them, not a face, but a whole body, cloaked in black.

Tala turned and fled into the crypt. The darkness enveloped her as she searched desperately for a hiding place, or better yet, an escape. The crypt was solid rock, names and dates etched at regular intervals. On the right, the rock disappeared into nothing, a gaping darkness, and Tala realised there were stairs going down. But where did they lead? Was there a way out?

She turned quickly back to the entrance, searching for the face. Terror flooded her in adrenaline, her heart pumping. What did he want with her?

She turned back to the stairs, but too quickly, and her foot slipped on the smooth rock, sending her tumbling down into the darkness.

***

HER CHEEK WAS COLD. IT WAS AGAINST SOMETHING COLD. And her body hurt, but especially her head. She reached a hand up to touch her forehead, then remembered. Eyes flying open, she saw... nothing. Darkness on all sides. But where were the stairs? Then a yellow light floated towards her. A firefly. Right?

She squeezed her eyes shut, breathing deeply. She had to stop her mind from spinning. It was this place... not her. She let her breath out as slowly as she could through her nose. She had to get out of this place and start thinking more rationally.

She opened her eyes. Staring at her, from the centre of the yellow light hovering in front of her nose, was a tiny, perfect face. She froze, goosebumps racing up her arms and down her spine.

The face was the calmest thing she had ever seen, and she couldn't look away. It was attached to a miniature body and what appeared to be fly's wings, beating rapidly.

The face smiled at her, then held out a hand no bigger than a mouse's, took a deep breath, and blew some glowing light onto Tala's nose. Immediately her body relaxed.

"Do not be afraid," the words seemed to radiate from the back of her head, then glowed through her brain, warming her and numbing the pain.

The fairy, she could think of no other word for the little creature, gestured in front of Tala's knees. Her phone. She picked it up gratefully and stood. The fairy waved her arms forward, beckoning Tala to follow, then turned towards the darkness and winked out.

Gone.

Of course.

Still, the sense of calm and warmth remained, and she took a few steps forward, the direction the fairy had gone. Complete and utter darkness.

Her phone! She flicked on the flashlight, and the glaring whiteness obliterated everything. Quickly dimming the light, she thought she heard a muffled step in front of her. She shone the light towards the stairs she had tumbled down, but there was only a solid wall of cold bricks and occasional etched graves markers. She turned behind her, another wall, cobwebs and stunted weeds attesting to the permanence of its existence. The stairs had vanished, and she was in a dead end.

"Do not be afraid," the voice in her head assured her, as she moved forwards down the dark hall. This place seemed much bigger than it looked from the graveyard. A place of death and memory. And maybe magic.

At the end of the hall, her light glinted off something in a small alcove. She reached forward and felt the cold metal of an urn, tarnished and oxidized with age. Rubbing it gently, she saw a shadow move suddenly across its surface. Whirling around, she gasped. The cloaked face! He was moving, gliding, smoothly towards her. But where had he come from? She gulped, adrenaline flooding her thoughts... *Run!*

Her phone tumbled to the ground, but she left it, running up a staircase that had somehow materialized and into a grassy twilit meadow she had not noticed before. There were white birch trees, and in front of them...

She caught her breath, the woman from her dream, the crouched woman holding a sleeping child.

Footsteps behind her. She turned again. Do not be afraid.

"Who are you?"

The cloaked face circled around her, giving her space, she thought, but she turned with him, watching, ready... he moved slowly and smoothly under the trees and towards the woman.

But it wasn't a woman. It was a statue. A grey stone angel holding a sleeping child.

And there were yellow lights floating gently around the meadow.

The cloaked figure stopped beside the statue and slowly, deliberately removed a mask, pulling the cloak off his head. It took her a moment.

"Ben?"

"Aye," he said quietly. "I didn't mean to scare you. I just kind of wanted to encourage you to come here..." A yellow light drifted onto his shoulder.

"What?" she had trouble finding words. "What is this place? Who are you? What do you mean 'encourage me'? You scared me half to death! Is this your sick idea of a joke?" Then warily, "are you following me?"

The yellow light drifted off his shoulder, and slowly came towards Tala. Once again she saw the perfect face, the tiny glowing being, and inside her head one overwhelming thought, "Don't fear, you are safe."

"I'm Ben," he smiled, and suddenly he was just the friendly youth from the inn. "I'm also kind of a messenger. I help people like you who come here… lost. Or looking for something."

"Me? What do you know about me?"

"Oh, sorry… I mean. I thought you were looking for something…" He walked towards the angel statue and put his hand almost lovingly on her head.

Tala stepped forward, "I had a dream about her…" she trailed off, not sure how to continue.

"Aye. I know. I was there… in a manner of speaking."

"You were there? In my dream? What do you mean?" she felt dizzy.

He looked up at her, pausing. "Your mother knew you were close. She has been looking for you."

"My… my mother?"

"Aye. I don't mean to get your hopes up. She is no longer here, but she wanted to send you a message."

Tears sprang into Tala's eyes, "My mother was here?"

"Aye, and her mother before her. She has been a part of the realm for longer than I know."

The yellow lights circled, seeming to spiral in an undulating dance, reaching towards Tala, without actually coming closer. The birch trees glowed in their light, and in the deepening purple sky. This place was alive, Tala noticed. The grass swayed gently though there was no breeze. Birds hopped in the branches, twittering happily, small creatures scurried in the tall grass.

The realm.

This is the place she had come to.

The tears slipped unnoticed down her cheek.

"And the message? What is her message to me?"

"You are safe here," he started. "This place is here whenever you need it." His words echoed the assurances the fairy had given her, the warm thoughts comforting her even now.

"Your mother never wanted to leave you. She wanted to return for you and bring you here, but... she couldn't. There are rules. And she needed us, but sometimes time does not work the same in our realm, and it makes it more difficult to return..."

"She wanted you to know, the fear in you, and the anger... it's not yours. It's not your fault. You were left in a hard place, and you have every right to feel angry, but the anger does not belong to you, and you can put it down. The world of men can plant these seeds in you, but you can also unplant them."

Tala stepped towards the statue, her attention drawn to the expression on the face of the mother, the pure tenderness and care towards her sleeping child.

"Your mother loves you," He put his arms around the statue, and Tala felt herself drawn in. She saw her mother as she had in her dream, but the sleeping child was her. She was cradled safely in her mother's arms. She was safe and loved. She felt whole.

"Anger is the fear of being lost," Ben continued. "You are not lost any more."

"This place we're in, it's a gateway. From here you can enter the realm, and it is always a safe place you can come to. But... you must be careful about the time thing..."

Tala looked up at Ben. "You're not really a teenager, are you?"

He smiled. "Not exactly. Come, take my hand."

Tala reached out, and Ben gently placed her hand on the angel's head and covered it with his own. As the world she knew shifted and melted away, Tala felt her fear also melting. She had found her mother. She was home.

.

Hürantån Helper

By Nick Forster

THE DAY ARRIVED WITHOUT SIGN OF DREAD: birdsong in the air, wind rustling the palms, and a small dog's bark. Yet Brooke squirmed with anxiety. Concern for her reckless daughter Coral in the big-wave competition consumed her like fire. With her curly brown hair blowing in the breeze, she sipped her coffee on the balcony, gripping the porcelain cup with white knuckles.

Coral had stopped answering her calls, likely sick of her mother's nagging. Certain death lay beneath the crashing water. It didn't matter she'd done it many times before, or that she led the pack in the Frontier Generation pro-circuit riders. Brooke knew all this, yet she tried one more time, hitting the implanted communications control high on her neck, right below her ear.

"Coral, it's your mother. Please answer."

The tone sounded more desperate than intended. The lack of reply and only sound resembled that of an empty Conch shell. The hollow, roaring hum of the surf echoed in her eardrum. Brooke strained her ears and pled once more to the emptiness. "Coral! You don't have to do this. You are not your father!"

Scott Blake refused to give up his childlike ways. Even at fifty-five, he didn't quit. Surfing huge waves, a vagabond travelling the planet, following that Xero Nekton like a lovesick puppy. Xero and the rest of the Hürantåns hid no longer, and for the past twenty years, they led the vanguard of world-change, fostering Humankind into a new era of responsible living. Advanced technology and social upheaval transformed Earth, and to the Frontiers, they were nothing short of gods. For Brooke, they were the same aliens who abducted her and had turned things upside down, making her life a circus of drugs and breakdowns.

Without warning, a tightness bound Brooke's chest and neck and her field of vision narrowed. Breath escaped her, and she dropped her cup, spilling the roasted Kenyan Java all over her legs before the concrete smashed the fragile vessel to bits. She gripped the metal edge of the black, cast-iron table beside her and fought the dizzying gravity.

After the events surrounding Coral's birth—the abductions, the otherworldly experiences—she'd experienced this panic regularly. The extreme, feel-like-you're-dying moments. Alcohol, drugs, therapy...

nothing helped abate them. The last trip off-world had been the worst, and she hadn't been the same since. She showed the typical symptoms of intergalactic-worm-hole travel, they said.

The Hürantåns, the colonizers, were once again Lords of the Earth, or Mowata as they called it, but this time there was full disclosure their origin was the watery planet Hürantå, far off in the Jergarcian Galaxy. For millennia, they posed as deities, performing miraculous feats, unsuccessfully steering humans away from disaster. Brooke cursed her ailment, for it meant the aliens' constant presence in her life, helping her to control her attacks and deal with her failure as a mother. The blue pills the medical attendant Jo-Loo provided subdued her moods, dousing the fire within, creating a lethargy that lasted for days. She had used them with devotion for at least a decade, leaving her soul an empty husk, allowing Jo-Loo to raise Coral, along with the semi-absent Scott, who despite a minor drinking problem, seemed to be annoyingly free of space sickness.

There was one pill left, in the top drawer where it had sat lonely for years.

The past flashed back to her as she held herself from falling. *"I don't want to have anything to do with them anymore!"* *Her words, sounding shrill to her own ears, pierced the dim-lit room of their small apartment above the marina.* *"They have left my life in shambles, stolen your attention, and turned my daughter into a thrill-seeking daredevil."*

Scott's tanned face betrayed his lack of comfort. He hated confrontation and talking about emotions and feelings was like having hairs plucked. *"But sweetie, they saved us. Look at our world now, the free power they've given and the direction... without them we'd have either killed ourselves off in a nuclear war or drowned in pollution. The Earth was on fire, for Pete's sake!"*

The cry of a gull snapped Brooke back to the present. Anxiety and fear pecked, and the old ghosts flocked. She was a bad mother. Absent and afraid. A failure. Scott's feeble attempt at parenting and her sickness forced them to enlist Hürantån help. Without their care, where would she be? What would have happened to Coral? They called her the prophesied one who would save Mowata, and she did.

But she doesn't have to risk her life today.

The muscles in Brooke's chest cramped and bound her ribs like a straightjacket. *I can't call Jo-Loo. The aliens started all this, and because of it, I'm a basket case, a disaster of a human.* Her heart raced, and her breathing shallowed, rivulets over a dried streambed evaporating on the hot rocks.

Hitting the button behind her ear, she screamed, "Scott,, are you there? Where are you?"

Only silence replied. The familiar void offering no panacea to her lunacy. He was gone, just like he'd been for the past twenty years.

I can't call them. I'm sick of them and all they've caused in my life.
The pill. I need it.

She'd worked hard to stop using and to reduce her reliance on outside help. The teachings of Henry David Thoreau helped: a quest for nothingness and a focus on mindfulness. All flew out the window when she was in this state. She had saved one pill, and Brooke slunk to the floor and crawled to the bedroom, clawing towards it like it was her only hope.

Even though it was of Hürantån origin, she had no choice. Her world crashed, cascading around her head. Soon it would bury her alive.

Inside the closet, up the built-in unit she climbed. At the top, the drawer slid open. The container at the back under the socks waited for her. Her breathing steadied, as if she'd overcome the attack without it, but the hunger awakened couldn't stop. With shaking fingers, she ripped off the lid of the canister and gasped.

The pill, now a puddle in the bottom of the tin, oozed and evaporated greenish-blue vapour after contact with the air. The tendrils rose, mocking her in her failure.

"No!" Brooke banished the instant desire to lick up the goo and slammed the useless metal box to the floor. "Why is this happening!" Dejected, she sank down to the ground and shook.

Breathe, Brooke, breathe. Call in Plan B. Call Jo-Loo. You have no choice.

Her vision blurred and the blackness closed in, she touched the neck controls again and opened the comm link. Although their globule-enclosed habitations had now spread throughout the planet and the moon, and new-comers from Hüranta freely mingled with the Frontier-gens. Jo-Loo lived in Pacificas, the Hürantån stronghold below the sea, where Brooke had first encountered the humanoid aliens.

"Jo-Loo, it's me. Coral's going to die. The attacks... they're happening again. I have none left. Please help."

After the words leaked out, she withdrew into a fetal position on the floor. Her spine curled, protecting her from the world, though it was her mind that plagued her with thoughts of doom and despair.

The reply didn't take long. Sparks of cyan and showering silver appeared in the room. A jet-black disc opened within the shimmering display, an opening, a portal between Pacificas and her bedroom. The shapeless, humanoid form of Jo-Loo, five-foot five, short blue hair with a kind, plain face, stepped through the teleportation rift. Never sure if Jo-Loo was male or female, Brooke associated their kindness and caring as female, although their features betrayed an affinity for neither. Although she first resisted calling them, relief and hope arrived with the Hürantån.

Jo-Loo dressed in a loose-fitting pastel garment, covering tight black pants. Behind, a Hürantån guard followed. Scott had named the security officers "unitards" because of the stretchy grey suits they wore, and this one did not differ. The lumpy brute towered above Jo-Loo, and his face, the only skin visible, revealed a dim-witted, toothy grin. The unitard tempered Brooke's initial relief, bringing memories of her captivity and the multiple worm-hole trips between Jergarcia and the Milky Way.

A dry croak escaped her lips, "Help," and then words followed, a babble of unattached nomenclature. Labels and sounds, fragments of sentences.

"Coral... The pill... ruined... She's doing it... didn't listen. Nowhere else. Nothing."

Jo-Loo's left eyebrow raised, and they reached down to touch Brooke's fetal form. Brooke recoiled from the contact. Intention clear in her mind, but the words came out a garbled mess.

"One thing at a time, sah Blake, please. I'm here now."

The concern in the alien's eyes brought back a flood of memories. Coral was an infant and Brooke could not cope, the look of pity on Jo-Loo's face as they took over maternal duties. Her failure to be a mother haunted her, as did her inability to be a successful, functioning human in this new world she'd fought so hard to save.

"Brooke, it's okay, you can tell me."

The words stung, and Brooke abandoned reality. The room spun and the colors melted. Refracted light twisted her vision and the outline of Jo-Loo stretched like a Gumby doll. The unitard, now an orangutan, grew and became disfigured. But her reflection in Jo-Loo's concerned eyes revealed a cornered animal with pupils the size of dinner plates and all colour drained from her face.

"NO! You did this to me. You, Hürantåns! Why me? Why us? Coral can't sit still because of you. She won't stop risking her life. She'll die today!

Don't touch me!"

The event took over, and she lost all control. She sprang from the floor and backed into the closet, causing the hanging garments to fall. She grabbed a wooden hanger off the rack and swung it at the advancing aliens. The unitard in her eyes was nothing but a grey menacing shape with outstretched claws.

"Calm down, Brooke, we are here to help. You called me, remember?"

Beyond reason, Brooke dodged under the unitard and reached the bureau where she grabbed a soapstone sculpture. She turned and flung it at her perceived attackers. "Stop where you are!"

Unfazed by the attack, the unitard was upon her, enveloping her in a tight embrace, his salty musty scent overpowering her senses. She struggled to no avail and felt a sharp prick in the back of her shoulder. Instant relief and calm gave way and the fight left her as she slumped into the guard's hold.

Jo-Loo withdrew the needle. "You are not safe by yourself and need to recover. Please understand I'm doing this for you. To help you, Brooke Blake. I'm taking you to the ship."

The tranquillizer's quick, all-encompassing effect reduced Brooke to a sentient ragdoll. Clarity returned to her mind with the immediacy of a bucket of water to the face. *I had a panic attack, my last pill, spoilt. I called Jo-Loo in desperation, and her appearance caused the craziness. Now I'm the puddle of goo.*

"Come, Brooke, we go."

She spoke as though Brooke had an option, and after touching her own comm pad, a sparking portal opened again, and the unitard stepped into the void with Brooke in his arms.

A free-fall of sorts ensued, and feeling of timeless emptiness engorged her as they streamed in a blink of an eye to an unfamiliar setting. Sterile metal walls surrounded them, with black open views to a star-filled expanse. Right before them a white apparatus sprang from the floor, and out of that tube, conduits and wires and smaller tubes snaked out in a twisting flowering mass, under which a bed-like platform emerged.

Oh no! The tube tree!

Brooke had seen it before and knew what it was all about. Unable to resist or move a muscle, her internal struggle produced nothing. Her eyes remained open even as her mind screamed, *"No! Not that. Please no, Jo-Loo!"*

But she had no control, and the words did not emerge. The unitard lay her down on the gurney, and the tubes and wires snaked around her, tipped with sharp needles that inserted themselves in her arms and neck and legs. Vision escaped her now, and the hollow feeling returned as her surroundings blurred. White light pulsed, and the caring face of Jo-Loo dominated her peripheral as the drugs took effect and the tubes invaded her mouth, nostrils and elsewhere.

An uneasy nothingness on the heels of sleep finally came.

The black hole of unconsciousness peppered with segments of dream took Brooke away from the panic. Time ceased to make sense, and fragments appeared in her mind. Unlike natural dreams, the visions resembled a slide show: brief, episodic, and unrelated stills. Scenes from Hürantå, of Pete, the battle for the consortium, and the killing of Wol zipped through her frontal cortex along with memories buried and long forgotten. She saw her mom helping sell lemonade on a hot summer day, first water polo practice in the fall on the new team, and the morning she was told her grandfather died.

The tubes retreated, and the wires withdrew. Fresh and awake, Brooke sat up on the gurney, and with returned strength, she stood. She found herself lucid and serene.

"I'm good," she said, and Jo-Loo and the other attendants turned to face her. "I'm good now, I'd like to go."

With a clear head, she took stock of her environment and noticed she wasn't the only one. At least a hundred other humans occupied the ship, hooked to the mechanical intravenous delivery and removal systems. An overall acceptance and knowledge that this was — a complete turn from her state of being upon arrival — overcame her. And it came as no surprise or fear that others were here. The round room spanned eighty feet in diameter, oval windows rimming the outer wall, and tube trees and gurneys ringing the space. In the middle at a circular dais, Jo-Loo and a group of similar-dressed attendants monitored a cast of coloured screens.

"These are others that needed our help too, Brooke," Jo-Loo said. "You are not the only one of our former specimens that requires assistance from time to time."

Brooke inhaled and surveyed the room with composure. She took a step forward while she contemplated her response. "I'm good," she repeated. "I'm good to go back."

Jo-Loo regarded her with a measured glance and compassion in her eyes. "Please, I know it's part of the sickness, but you must trust us, the pills are the best way to combat what afflicts. If you maintain the dosage, situations like this should not occur."

Brooke exhaled and let her shoulders drop. She released all the animosity toward the Hürantån and feelings of love and gratitude filled her. Jo-Loo had been nothing other than caring and helpful, from the first time she saw them on the *Osiris*, to how they had been there for Coral all those years.

"Coral."

Brooke's senses lit as she remembered her daughter. But the compounds washing through her enabled her to react with peacefulness and calm, replacing the turmoil she felt earlier.

"The big wave competition is today," Brooke blurted. "Can you teleport me there, please?"

Jo-Loo tilted her head and a sympathetic light shone within. "You realize you can't stop her, Brooke. It's her choice, and the anxiety is not helpful."

Brooke closed her eyes and then opened them. "Thank you, Jo-Loo, but I want to watch. I know I can't stop her now, it's just, I need to be there."

Jo-Lo smiled, a rare brightness of face that transformed plain features into a beautiful beacon. Bending down, they rustled below the counter and pulled out a new tin. The contents shifted as they held it out to Brooke. "I'm glad you agree, Brooke. I'm sending you off with more pills. Promise me you'll take one a day to stave off the attacks. It's the only way."

Brooke reached out and grabbed the tin. "Thank you, I will. But please, I'm good now, and I would like to see my daughter."

Jo-Loo nodded and handed Brooke the medicine. Surety, comfort, and safety took the form of a heavy, rattling pill container, and for the first time that day, a smile crept across Brooke's face.

"Ok, Brooke, we'll send you to the competition. Your daughter is about to compete."

Brooke said her goodbyes and took one last glance at the spaceship, with its rows of human patients and attending unitards with the views to space. Somehow, she accepted the strangeness of it all, as if it were no more than a scene at her local park. She'd seen it all before, of course, and stranger things. The Human Elite hooked up inside the transport globules in the Hotel Armada came to mind, as did the assembly hangar on Hüranta when the globules were loaded on the *Osiris*.

These scenes did not bother her now, evoked no more of a response than a nostalgic tweak. The compounds from the tube tree were similar yet stronger to the daily buzz of the blue pills she'd known for years. The weight of the fresh supply in her pocket felt reassuring. She turned her back on the floating hospital space asylum and nodded to the portal master.

"Maverick beach, please," she said as calm as if talking to a city bus driver.

"Right this way, sah Blake," the portal master said, and ushered her to the raised dais. With familiar flash and spark, Brooke stepped into the black. Her molecules, like confetti in a blender, swished and swirled as if in a massive Electrolux and sucked down to the beach.

A stiff wind whipped back her hair and her loose-fitting shirt, straining the outline of the pill container in her cotton shorts just above the coffee stain. The portal plunked her down on the edge of the dune where below, a crowd stood with rapt attention facing the raging sea. Dark blue and purple mountainous shapes shifted and grew and fell and churning white water foam mingled with the rocky shore.

"Our next rider is the one and only Coral Blake, from Hawaii-Huran team, ranked fifth in the big-wave circuit."

The man spoke through a megaphone, and his amplified voice floated up over the crowd and through the marram grass and past Brooke's ears. The breeze shifted, and the banter muffled, but Brooke caught the words "fearless" and "aggressive style" and snippets of the crowd's cheers.

Brooke sipped the wind and looked out to the break. The currents converged on the point, where a wide brown cliff jutted like the prow of a mighty vessel, driving into the North Pacific as the full might of its power broke on its shores. These were no lap waves, or gentle rollers. The lesser of the competition waves, the ones too small for consideration towered over the cliffs as they rushed toward landfall. Millions of cubic feet of H2O, seemingly angry at the land, threw themselves with all their might, pounding the rock and reef into sand and submission.

Far on the break, a black speck appeared. A jet pod sped up the shoulder of a massive heavy, towing none other than her daughter. She could see the red shirt like a beacon. This was it, and it was happening. With not even a raise in heartbeat, Brooke watched as if she were watching something as benign as a chess match between two strangers. Forgotten were the tears and theatrics of the morning.

Above the wave on the horizon, a sparkle as a Hürantån skimmer ship took off from the ocean. Over the past twenty years they'd rid the oceans of last century's garbage. Scott and Dr. Stevens discovery of the Peterplankton helped, a species of plastic-eating plankton that broke down plastic into composite parts, but the Hürantån spaceships sped the process. *Why did I resent these beings?* Perhaps it was the compound running through her veins, but she put the doubt and the past behind her. The Hürantåns were here to help. They'd done what she'd rallied for, cleaned the oceans, and steered Humankind away from greed and overconsumption, albeit sometimes with a heavy hand. She took a deep breath and followed the skimmer's rise through the atmosphere toward Moon Base One. She let go of any last vestige of anxiety and watched with a chemical-induced smile on her lips. Her only daughter, the great Coral Blake, prophesied savior of Mowata, pro-extreme surfer, and celebrity to the Frontier Generation set out on a two hundred-foot mountain of moving water.

The crowd stood silent now, the megaphone hung at the man's side. Coral's tiny form in the distance dropped like a rocket, the point of her board cutting through the water and sending up spray. Perhaps it was a pocket of clean blood, or just too much for the drugs to handle, because a pit opened in Brooke's gut, and fear struck her to her core. She recalled the memory of her husband on the back of the Hürantåguan—Godzilla on steroids—Scott clinging to a scale as it smashed into the waters of Hürantå like an asteroid. She clutched the pill box through her shorts as the gigantic wave curled over top of Coral and an avalanche of furious white water showered down just behind her as she flew down the watery slope.

Like a bad movie, the scenes plagued her. The Hürantåguan. Eigor Gutt. The wormholes and the Squidarma. The drugs kept her on point though, as she remained fixated on the race of daughter vs nature unfolding before her eyes. If she fell now, she'd be smashed to pieces by a billion tons of water.

She pictured that day on the beach. The rocks at Argentia and being saved from the thrashing Shagarks. The wild chase through the streets of Hürantå City around and through the pods surrounding the domed power centre. It was hard to consider anything more powerful than the liquid gargantuan wall of water towering above Coral, but still Brooke watched. Images of her lost motherhood years plagued her. The inability to cope and the refusal to get help. Fighting the uncontrollable and resisting the aid offered to her. She gripped the pill container and vowed never to let them run dry again. She'd fought the Hürantån help, held onto her humanity, though chunks of it had been crushed in the travels through space.

A small tear escaped her eye even as the crowd hushed and the wind stilled. Coral's trajectory turned and with a burst of speed and a mighty wallop, the rest of the curling beast smashed down on top of her. Those assembled gasped and several screamed. The roiling waters bubbled and churned and the rescue pods zoomed in.

Brooke closed her eyes. *This is what you were scared of. The death of your daughter. Why aren't you freaking, Brooke?* She held her breath. *Is this drug worth it, to hide your pain... your feelings... your humanity?*

And the empty shell of her life crashed down around her, just as the mighty wave had smashed down on her only daughter. A delayed shriek left her lungs and pierced through the wind. "Coral!"

"Don't leave us!" She fell to her knees and buried her head in her hands. She could hear the rescuers zigzagging through the chop and the murmurs of the crowd. Brooke felt the cold nuzzle of a wet nose on her thigh. A brown and white puppy had found her in the long grass. She picked it up and held it to her breast.

"What are you doing here, little one?"

She shifted to a sitting position and cuddled the stray dog, his paws standing half on her leg, half on the pill box tucked safely in her pocket.

Just Another Brick in the Wall

By Ron Wild

SISYPHUS LIMPED TOWARDS TOWN; tattered dirty clothes, scratches bleeding, calloused hands, sunburnt skin. Migrants often passed near or through this town, but no one paid them much attention. In this case however, Sisyphus intended to stay awhile. Little did the townspeople know the great contribution he would make during his stay. Mason heard rumours about the newcomer but hadn't yet seen him around town. As a busy construction worker, Mason was focused on making a contribution towards the building of a great new cathedral in town.

The process of laying bricks and blocks had not really advanced much over thousands of years. It is still very much manual labour, albeit with a fairly high skill and experience requirement. Each component is handled once, typically by an individual mason. He picks up a single brick and butters the mortar on the two end faces. Next, the brick is carefully placed in line with the row of the wall being built. Often string lines are tied across to help ensure that the row is perfectly level. Decisive tapping with the trowel handle pushes the brick down into the soft mortar to exactly the prescribed level. Excess mortar is scraped off with the trowel and placed on top of the row where the next brick will be laid.

Pride in his work was what Mason valued most. He couldn't imagine ever having to compromise that deeply held personal value. Every brick he laid, on every row, in every wall, was placed with the utmost attention and care. Every day he enjoyed the fruits of his labours, knowing that the building owner and its future inhabitants would appreciate his workmanship for many decades to come. Mason was proud of being one of the best bricklayers in the local guild.

A spray of stars blazed in the night sky. They provided just enough light for overnight travel. Sisyphus always walked alone and could make his way steadily even with minimal starlight or moonshine. He liked to travel at night when it was cooler. Working all day long under the blazing sun made him really look forward to the nighttime walking. The cool breeze felt particularly refreshing against his sunburnt face and neck.

This journey was typical of many he had taken whenever it was time to relocate from one town to the next. He usually didn't reside in any one place for more than a changing of the seasons. It seemed like a quarter-year or two gave him a town-life experience that suited his needs and interests. As he walked along the road in the dark, the stars were truly inspiring. He was happy to be in transit again. The last town experience was productive in his estimation, but relatively uneventful. As always, he spent his days rolling boulders up mountain sides. The whole past year was no different in that respect. Or the years before that. The townspeople generally left him alone once they confirmed that he was indeed harmless. No one understood his passion for relocating large boulders to higher ground, but since he wasn't harming anyone in the process, people let him be. The town he was leaving was situated in a valley among gently rolling foothills, and Sisyphus was excited about moving upstream in the direction of higher hills. Mountainous terrains always attracted his notice, as he was energized by the greater challenge provided. On steeper mountains he had to consider the number of switchbacks his boulder-rolling path would have to follow. Too many back-and-forths would increase the distance he had to push a boulder. Too few meant he would exhaust himself without making significant vertical progress. Sisyphus intuitively experimented with several different slope and distance combinations. While not well-versed in geometry or physics, he was able to gauge his personal effort expenditures in raising the potential energy of his beloved boulders.

A new town and the mountains surrounding it, provided exciting new opportunities for him. However, walking between towns was a real treat because he didn't have to push a boulder all the way. Walking on relatively level land felt good for a change. His aching back and leg muscles appreciated the reprieve from steep-slope traversing. As he walked, Sisyphus imagined what the next town might be like. It usually wasn't a problem finding appropriately sized boulders for his purpose. It was typically the mountainside conditions that provided the greatest challenge. Too much vegetation would make his task more difficult, while a bald mountain would leave him exposed to the blazing sun all day long. Looking up at the star-filled sky, he was grateful for the light provided without oppressive heat.

***

MASONRY IS VERY PHYSICALLY DEMANDING WORK. While each individual brick may only weigh a few pounds, a man will hoist hundreds of pounds per day, and tons over the course of his working career. Repetitive strain wrist and shoulder problems are common in the trade. The work requires climbing high scaffolds and standing all day on them. Many short steps are taken back and forth to the brick pile and mortar pail. Standing all day long is another occupational requirement. Sore hips and knees are common, especially as a man gets older. Most masonry work is performed outdoors, frequently in the blazing sun. Job sites are busiest in the morning before the heat of the day makes conditions unbearable. Typically, masonry work is halted well before any rain falls because mortar must not become over-saturated.

Winter weather is not conducive to quality masonry construction. Severe structural problems can result if mortar freezes before it has time to cure properly. During freezing temperature periods, masons can do support activities or indoor projects instead. Most men were furloughed for at least three or four months per year. Typically, they were sufficiently well paid while working, to ensure the necessary cash flow to survive rather comfortably through to spring. Seasonality was a feature of their profession that most masons actually appreciated. Many took on other less physically demanding work during the construction off-season. They looked forward to a chance to rehabilitate their aching muscles.

One day the gossip around the cathedral jobsite was concerning a wall that had collapsed on the outskirts of their town. Rumours were flying about the cause of the disaster, and who was to blame. A structural collapse like that was a catastrophic event that fortunately, rarely occurs. Everyone in the construction industry is disturbed by such news, especially when it occurs in the vicinity of where they have previously worked. Each man tries to remember the particular structure and his personal role in building it. Work done in poor weather is often suspect. Too often a workman's discomfort affects his decision-making and care and attention. That's when shoddy work usually happens, and is rarely noticed, let alone remediated or replaced.

Whenever a wall collapses, the building owner calls for an investigation into the cause. In larger projects a full inquiry is held to determine responsibility and legal liability. The offending workers and lax inspectors can even face criminal charges if negligence is determined. Every construction worker hoped to avoid finding themselves in such a predicament. The first words that flashed through Mason's mind were, "It can't be my fault!" A workplace accident such as a wall collapse draws attention to past deficiencies in labour quality. Taking great pride in his workmanship prevented Mason from even considering the possibility that he could ever have produced substandard work. Aware of the career-ending consequences of such a charge, he grew keenly interested in this matter.

Mason took more pride in his work than many of his fellow bricklayers. The older ones in particular seemed to cut corners and work sloppily. Those in the know could tell who laid which rows of bricks. Mason prided himself in being one of the best. He wasn't the fastest, nor was he the slowest. He just paid the most attention, and deeply cared about a job well-done. Whether they were building a castle or a barn, Mason worked with the very same focused effort. He believed that each brick should be handled like a precious treasure.

Occasionally there were problems on the construction worksite. An inspector could flag any work that was not up to specifications. Theoretically, the offending bricklayer would have to demolish the unsatisfactory work and rebuild it properly on his own time at his own expense. This had never happened to Mason, and he couldn't bear the thought of producing substandard work. While he could shoulder the criticism of his fellow guild members, the shame of telling his family about his plight would be his worst nightmare.

Stone walls have protected castles and towns for centuries. They have withstood all manner of attack, natural and man-made. Very few walls have ever been breached in any way. A brick wall was also considered a strong fire-proof roof support, and protection for all living within those walls. This disaster drew all those historical beliefs into question. "Are walls all of a sudden inadequate for some reason?" Are bricklayers not the admirable constructors they once were? Is Mason's profession suddenly suspect, or worse, obsolete for some reason?"

After getting over the initial emotional shock, everyone's natural reaction was, "No... Other parties must be to blame." The first suspects were typically the providers of faulty building materials. Being lower on the supply chain hierarchy, the brick-makers were the first to be scrutinized. They were generally untrained and poorly supervised. Maybe they used the wrong clay for that batch of bricks? Maybe they added too much water to the slurry? Or not enough? Perhaps the oven was running too hot? Or not hot enough, rendering the bricks brittle? Minute cracks would go unnoticed. Only later the water from the mortar mixture might cause problems during the wall-building process. However, over many outdoor seasonal freeze-thaw cycles, moisture tends to absorb through small cracks. It would expand during the winter causing the crack to be permanently opened wider.

Once the materials and their producers were roundly criticized, attention would turn to the possibility of a faulty initial structural design. Even well-placed strong bricks could crumble if the building architect had errored. Undue tension forces could not be accommodated by bricks intended for compression use only. Maybe the design had spans that were too long, or unsupported heights that would be inherently unstable? Innovative architects have been known to push materials and technologies to the breaking point. Perhaps someone had used the traditional materials in innovative yet-unproven ways?

***

FEW YOUNG MEN VALUED THEIR VOCATION as much as Mason did. He grew up in a family of five children, all boys, and he was the youngest. His older brothers had excelled in school and gone on to professional careers. Mason, on the other hand, had chosen the vocational route, training to be a bricklayer. While he really loved working with his hands on construction sites, his family was not particularly supportive of his career choice. Mason always felt conscientious of the fact that they were generally disappointed in him.

Luckily Mason found support among his fellow bricklayers. They were all members of a masonry guild that upheld work standards in their field. Mason was a proud member of the guild working to meet or exceed all the performance requirements. The one thing he valued above all else was pride in his work. In addition to working quickly, he strove to be very precise in the laying of each and every brick that he handled. He made sure his rows were perfectly straight, forming walls that were perfectly vertical. He was more careful than his contemporaries in mixing mortar that would cure exceptionally hard. This meant his mixture was thicker and more difficult to work with than the soupy mortar that others used. Even though he had to work harder as a result of this choice, he valued a finished product that would rank the highest quality among all the guild members.

There were concerns among the towns-folk that the collapsed wall had been built with shoddy workmanship and materials. They questioned whether the damage should be repaired, or the project abandoned. Within the masons' ranks there was defensive finger-pointing and scapegoating. The brotherhood spirit among guild members was under stress. Co-workers now looked at each other competitively. Mutual trust in workmanship quality had been shaken.

"You are hereby served notice to testify at the inquiry tomorrow."

With receiving that proclamation, Mason had been drawn into the thick of things. Always a proud bricklayer, Mason was actually eager to attend the inquiry meeting to learn what had happened and why. Who or what was at fault? What can be learned to prevent this type of failure in the future? Many fellow guild members were in attendance. Each had a theory, justification, or rationalization. Tension was running high as the assembled awaited the officials to take the stage.

"Walls have protected us from slings and arrows for centuries, but... in this case a boulder rolled down the mountain, crashing into the wall, demolishing it," summarized the judge. Earlier, the jobsite supervisor told how a boulder had come thundering down the mountain side, narrowly missing a school before crashing through the town border wall. Broken bricks and scaffolding had littered the area. Lucky no one was in the vicinity at the time of the crash. The damage could have been much more extensive. While this Sisyphus character was clearly negligent in allowing one of his boulders to smash into the wall, the inquiry was further trying to update their building standards. Was a boulder crash something they should be building to withstand in the future? Or was it a freak accident, like an act of God?

However, it had been the investigation into workmanship quality that was making all of the attendants nervous. The first on the stand was the head of the brick-making operation. He was grilled about the factory's equipment and his quality-control procedures. Investigators were trying to determine if faulty bricks were in fact partly to blame for the wall falling to pieces when the boulder struck it. The masonry personnel who worked on that particular part of the building were next to be questioned. The Master Mason explained that all his men did quality work, especially the younger crew that had built the part of the wall in question. After all his consternating Mason was relieved to learn that he was not required to testify on his behalf. Never before was there any need for him to verbally defend the quality of his workmanship. His record in that regard would continue unblemished.

The lead architect was queried next. Was their building design inadequate in any way? Could they reasonably be expected to design for a boulder strike of this magnitude? Should the code be updated to accommodate this type of applied force in the future?

By far what Mason found most interesting was the fact that Sisyphus was not present at the proceedings, nor required to testify. How could the individual responsible for this workplace accident be automatically exonerated of any wrongdoing? Or wouldn't he be the least bit curious about the inquiry, and attend voluntarily? Could he not interrupt his boulder pushing routine for a single day to attend the inquest? It seemed that Sisyphus was garnering preferential treatment even when he was a relative newcomer to the community. Mason found it curious that the culprit was given special treatment in this instance. Usually strangers were treated suspiciously until they established trustworthy relationships with townsfolk and their leaders. Who exactly was this mysterious man? Mason was motivated to learn more about him.

***

"EACH BRICK IS PRETTY MUCH THE SAME. I carefully lay them in neat rows, one on top of the last, day after day for years. This is the life of a bricklayer or stone mason." Mason actually thoroughly enjoyed his line of work as a bricklayer. Every day he added rows to walls which were forming castles, cathedrals or protective fortresses. He took great pride in placing each brick or block in exactly the right position. With the highest degree of care and attention, he repeated this task hundreds of times per day, all day, every day.

His brothers asked, "Don't you get bored with such repetitive tasks? Wouldn't you rather work in a nice comfortable office, rather than high on a scaffold in the burning sun or cold winds?" He actually found the routine to be quite relaxing, even fulfilling. Placing each brick with such care required his full attention. He lost all sense of time when he was in the flow of his work. He was often surprised when the workday came to an end; it felt like it had just started.

The Master Mason had given Sisyphus a guided tour of the construction site, explaining what each man was contributing to the project goal. He explained the pulley and winch systems that helped the men hoist heavy loads up to great heights. He pointed out the plumb lines that guided their work to a straight finish. All the way along, Sisyphus listened and looked carefully at what was presented, nodding frequently, seemingly in agreement.

The Master Mason also wanted Sisyphus to spend time with some of the other bricklayers under his command. He chose three that represented a cross-section that a newcomer would be expected to work with. Mason was the youngest of the men chosen. It was only then that Mason himself realized that he was considered by his boss to be an exemplary bricklayer. He felt proud to take time off the scaffolding to talk to a potential new recruit of his beloved profession. Mason tried to emphasize the advantage of masonry construction work over Sisyphus's full-time boulder rolling habit. He demonstrated the leverage provided by the pulley system that they used in their work. While it was still manual labour, it wasn't the back-breaking kind that Sisyphus experienced all day, every day on the mountainside. Sisyphus seemed intrigued by this new technology acknowledging that it would be a lot less physically demanding than what he was used to. Mason eagerly answered the few questions that Sisyphus posed about the physical demands of bricklaying. However, little was discussed regarding the rewarding Zen nature of mindful bricklaying.

Finally, Mason summarized, "In some ways the repetitiveness of bricklaying is similar to your endless rolling of boulders up the mountainside. However, we get the satisfaction of seeing brick rows grow up to be the walls of beautiful cathedrals and castles. Our work will be enjoyed by people for decades or centuries to come. There is something gratifying about that prospect. Every brick we lay is building a bigger dream. We can look back with pride at what we've constructed and say, 'I made that!' I don't understand how boulder pushing can be at all fulfilling for you, especially if it rolls back down right after all your hard work. At the end of the day, nothing has changed, a boulder lays in the valley, like it did the day before, and will tomorrow and the next day."

They gossiped around town that the King had been very upset with Sisyphus when the boulder crashed into the wall. Mason wondered how Sisyphus could return to his boulder-rolling activities after such a scolding. You'd think that a catastrophe would be enough to encourage a rational man to change his behaviour. The more time Mason spent with Sisyphus the more intrigued he was with him. Sisyphus was turning out to be a more complex character than the townspeople generally gave him credit for. When Mason felt obliged to get back to work, he returned Sisyphus to the Master Mason and bid him farewell.

In conclusion the Master Builder offered, "Bricklaying is a perfect vocation for anyone who finds satisfaction in repetitive outdoor work. Maybe you should consider becoming a mason, and joining our guild? You have lots of experience working outside with your hands. Bricks are easier to move and lift than the heavy boulders you've been pushing around. Brick by brick you can be part of building something at least as large, and usually much more impressive. Why don't you learn bricklaying skills by apprenticing with our guild?" Sisyphus paused to consider the Master Mason's proposal for a few moments. Shuffling uncomfortably, Sisyphus responded with surprising grace. He thanked the masons for building walls so straight and tall and strong... then Sisyphus went out and again started pushing a rock up the mountainside.

***

MASON WAS SURPRISED TO LEARN THAT SISYPHUS had rejected the career promotion opportunity so quickly. He thought that there must be lots that we don't know about Sisyphus' boulder rolling practice. The next day from high on the scaffold he saw Sisyphus on the ground pushing a boulder towards the mountain. He watched with considerably more attention than he ever had before. Sisyphus would strain against the boulder for a few minutes, then stop for a rest. Maybe he advanced a few feet. Again, he would lean his shoulder into the boulder trying to roll it further. Soon he stopped, exhausted, and wiped his brow with his calloused hand.

Turning his attention back to his own work, Mason carefully buttered a brick with mortar and placed it at the end of the row. There was great satisfaction in placing it precisely flat and straight. He looked down the row, and across the wall to see all that he had built today. Packing up at the end of the workday, Mason headed home with a great sense of accomplishment. He couldn't imagine working hard at anything that did not give him that positive feedback.

The more he thought about it on his walk home, the more Mason recognized similarities between bricklaying and boulder rolling. Basically, they were both outdoor forms of manual labor resulting in sunburned skin and blistered callused hands. Working with such heavy loads could really be 'back-breaking' labour, resulting in sore back and shoulder muscles. Elbow and wrist repetitive strain injuries were also common afflictions. Walking home at days end in their dirty tattered clothes, it was difficult to distinguish between the rock layers and boulder rollers.

Boulder pushing and bricklaying were both dirty jobs. They left a man covered in dust by day's end. Their clothing was likewise dirty and torn over time due to the nature of the work. These blue-collar activities actually left a grey ring of dirt around the cuffs and neck of their shirts. No fancy clean uniforms for either of these guys.

Upon reflection, the differences were more dramatic than the similarities. Both bricklayers and Sisyphus worked all day with stone or like materials. In fact, the larger blocks that masons occasionally set were typically chiseled out of a large boulder like ones Sisyphus rolled around. The blocks and bricks were typically smoother to the touch. They were smaller and much lighter in weight, more easily moved and lifted.

A large boulder was the base material for both Sisyphus and Mason. However, in Sisyphus's case, a raw boulder was all he needed. As long as it was naturally spherical enough to roll, it met his requirements. It wasn't that simple in the construction trade, however. Considerable processing effort was required to turn a boulder into blocks or bricks that could be stacked to form walls of buildings. The boulders' roundness was not a desirable feature, but rather one that needed to be overcome. A whole industry grew up devoted to turning round rocks into square ones. More resources were required to produce a perfectly square block, than would be spent later stacking them to form walls. In this respect the block and brick-makers were most important even though they occupied the bottom rung of the construction hierarchy.

Sisyphus labored all day long alone. He never spoke to anyone. Only when he started out from town in the morning did anyone even notice him. When he returned off the mountain at the end of the day, no one ever bothered to ask him how his day had been. They knew it had been the same as yesterday, and the day before that, for weeks and months on end. While bricklaying is a solitary task, it is typically done within a team of contemporaries. The men acknowledge each other and the work they are doing. They can chat idly without interfering with their work objectives. Even if a man preferred to work in silence, he still benefited from the background conversation noise on the scaffold.

As the tired bricklayers climbed down off the scaffolding at day's end they were frequently greeted by passing townspeople who marveled at what they had accomplished that shift. Rows of bricks became walls that started to inform the structure. Even younger children were able to see what was taking shape day by day. What once started as an ephemeral idea on paper, was now manifesting in real world brick and mortar. A castle or cathedral was in the process of taking its place in the cityscape. Most builders and constructors were generally held in fairly high regard by the communities who would benefit from their skill and effort. There would always be at least one wide-eyed boy watching carefully and dreaming of a future for himself as a builder.

Everyone in town had watched Sisyphus at one time or another. They saw him strain to push a heavy boulder up the mountainside slope. Frequently, they saw a boulder rolling right back down again to its original position. Sisyphus would trudge down to it, and start rolling it back up again. Once an observer had witnessed a few repetitions, they lost interest in watching Sisyphus any longer. It was just the same thing over and over. Occasionally they would notice him pushing up hill or walking back down to put his shoulder into a boulder to begin again. People quickly lost interest in what he might be up to. Gradually, Sisyphus became almost invisible in the eyes of his neighbours. It was only the great wall crash and inquiry that ever caused any notice.

Everyone just assumed that Sisyphus did not enjoy the same level of job satisfaction as the average worker. People watched with great suspicion every morning as he set out rolling another boulder towards the neighbouring mountain. 'Why would anyone want to do such a thing?' they wondered, 'day after day, in weather foul and fair. What motivated a capable man to waste his life in such pursuits?' Since they couldn't understand him, people generally walked wide circles around him, shaking their heads as they passed. Sisyphus knew he was mocked and joked about, but it didn't surprise or necessarily disappoint him. People generally under-appreciate what they don't understand.

***

DURING THE CONSTRUCTION PHASE, temporary scaffolding is erected to bring men and materials to the desired working height. On large cathedral projects, the scaffolding itself can be an engineering marvel. Over the centuries different materials have been employed, but the basic concepts remain the same. Bricklayers need a straight flat surface that they can stand and walk on. In addition to the weight of the work crew, the scaffolds need to support the bricks and mortars to be used to construct the wall. Generally, scaffolding was under-appreciated technology in the construction industry.

Another wall-building challenge was lifting the bricks and mortar to the heights that the men were currently working at. The hoisting effort could be considerable given the weight of the materials that need to be lifted. Pulleys and winches have been developed over the years to assist with this back-breaking work. Ramps were once tried but are rarely used anymore. Masonry was all straight-up vertical in orientation.

That fateful day all construction work was halted by the news that an army was advancing through the valley to attack their town. Ironically, some of the guild members were employed to build a fortress wall for just such an occasion. Masonry construction was generally a good security measure but required months of advance planning and years of onsite construction activity. A stone or brick wall could generally withstand all contemporary weaponry. Even rocks catapulted towards it at great velocity generally did surprisingly little damage. Since the walls were incomplete, the town's security forces had to take positions further back than they would have liked. That put their own catapulting weaponry out of range of the advancing enemy. Likewise, their traditional canons would be less effective at this longer range. The enemy clearly chose an opportune time for their attack. They planned to draw nearer to their target than was ever previously possible. The foe confidently marched up the valley unimpeded.

Unchallenged, yet surprised, the enemy exclaimed, "Their defence artillery is more deadly than we expected. They're sending boulders down upon us from all directions!" This surprise attack decimated their forces. Large boulders were rolling at them from on high, and afar, with considerable momentum. There was no stopping a boulder traveling at that speed. Both men and equipment were smashed beyond recognition by these unsophisticated munitions.

Back in town however, the fearful defence army was dreading a bloody battle. They had been caught in a very vulnerable position by this surprise attack. They could only watch in fear as the enemy advanced closer and closer. The commander issued an order to test the range of their equipment. Both a canon shot and a catapulted rock fell harmlessly short of where the enemy was expected to dig in. The commander feared the town was to be laid siege with tremendous loss of life and property damage. He was therefore shocked to see that the enemy suddenly stopped advancing towards them. In fact, they turned and started fleeing from whence they came. Commander could not believe his good fortune. One of his intelligence personnel reported from the frontlines that boulders had come reigning down from the peak that Sisyphus had been frequenting. With surprising accuracy, the boulders had been aimed at the enemy and discharged in their direction. Almost every boulder hit a combination of enemy soldiers and equipment. Very quickly, their ranks were decimated to the point that their leader called for a retreat. In panicked disarray they hurried back in the direction of their hometown defeated. They knew what hit them, but they didn't know who was responsible.

Word spread around town that the advancing enemy had been bombarded by boulders crashing down on them from an adjacent mountain peak. Only the community who had long watched the strange man in their midst suspected that Sisyphus was responsible for this heroic defensive maneuver. Of course, Sisyphus was the obvious protagonist. Who else was involved with boulders and mountains? Mason was gradually starting to appreciate what Sisyphus had been up to all this time.

Peering over an as-yet-unfinished wall, Mason could see a large crowd walking down the street towards him. He was surprised to see that in front of them was a Sisyphus-sized boulder. Groups of four or five men took turns pushing the boulder a few feet along. It was physically exhausting work that required a changing of the manpower every five minutes or so. Mason couldn't imagine how Sisyphus was able to push a boulder by himself, uphill, day after day as he did.

"Come down and join us! We are going to the top of the mountain to see the operation that Sisyphus has constructed there," they invited Mason. Pushing the boulder uphill required larger groups that changed-off more frequently. The celebratory crowd was certain that Sisyphus would be grateful for the gift boulder that would soon be presented to him. However, cresting the mountain peak they couldn't see any tower or munition magazines that they expected. In fact, on the mountain top they found no fortress, walls, or bricks, or boulders. And no Sisyphus.

Of course, various factions of the group were expecting to find something different at the peak. The architects were expecting to find a fortress from which Sisyphus could dispatch ammunition at the opposing foes. However, there was no evidence of any site facilities or master design of any kind. All the architect could point to was the likely spot from which Sisyphus had pushed boulders towards the foe in the valley below.

The masons were expecting to find impressive battlements but could not find evidence that anything had ever been built at all. There were certainly no fortress walls like the kind they took pride in building around their town. The brick-makers wondered what had become of all the boulders that Sisyphus had rolled up over the preceding weeks. They expected that someone would have taken some of those raw materials and made them into blocks or bricks, as they would naturally have done. To their surprise they found no sign of bricks, blocks, or boulders. The site was barren of any raw materials of any kind, or evidence of any construction activity.

The soldiers were thinking they might find a rogue militia of some kind posted at the mountaintop. How else could such a devastating assault have been launched against the attacking marauders? Despite their outfitting with equipment and supplies in town, the defence forces had proven to be far less effective than the mountain top phenomenon.

As the group surveyed the abandoned mountain-top site, neither did they find Sisyphus there as they had expected. His heroic activities were impressively unfathomable. Mason realized that they all underestimated Sisyphus and the efforts they had witnessed him expending. It dawned on them now why Sisyphus turned down every invitation to change his line of work. He didn't need a cushy job, or advanced tools, or a fancy work uniform to feel fulfilled in his vocation. Still Mason wondered how Sisyphus could predict that all the boulders he pushed up the mountain would ever prove useful. It was unlikely that he could have expected an advancing army attack. What else was he possibly thinking he could do with a pile of boulders on this mountain peak? Could he really have been gratified by the pushing routine alone? This whole episode gave Mason lots to think about. He now had a better appreciation of what motivates men. Each role is valuable in its own right.

Pointing west into the setting sun, someone shouted, "There he goes!" Mason squinted his eyes, finally focusing on Sisyphus limping toward the next town; tattered dirty clothes, scratches bleeding, calloused hands, sunburnt skin.

The Fallen

By Margaret Woodford

"ANITA, A DELIVERY CAME FOR YOU. It's a pretty decrepit-looking box, so I asked Bill to take it to the cellar," Mr. Page called from the doorway.

A frown crossed Anita's face. "A box for me? I wasn't expecting anything."

"A mysterious delivery? Well, it's definitely a box of books. Maybe mystery novels?" He chuckled at his own joke. "And they say library life is dull. Before you leave, could you unpack the new books that came today? They're behind the desk. Thanks. See you on Monday."

"Sure. Goodnight, Turner." She locked the door behind him and wandered through the stacks, caressing the spines of her charges. The ancient pine floor crooned beneath her soft-soled shoes. "The best part of the day and new books, too."

She raised the carton lid and inhaled the fresh ink smell. "*Mmm.* Delicious!" The pages whispered beneath her fingers. "Oh, yeah. Talk to me, my beauties!"

The floorboards groaned. "Bill, is that you? I thought you had left already." She scanned the room, but there was no one. Goosebumps prickled her arms. "This creaky old place." The setting sun gleamed through leaded glass scattering prisms across the polished floor. "It's getting late. I hate to leave you, but…" She stood up to stretch. "Maybe I'll have a quick peek at that box in the cellar."

"Turner was right, it is rather decrepit." Anita ran her fingers over the stiff brown wrapping paper and studied the label in the dim light. *A. Delaynie c/o Lance Cove Library.*

"No clue as to who sent it. Well, let's have a look-see."

The fusty paper disintegrated as she peeled back the yellowed tape. Anita sneezed and addressed the tiny particles that danced toward the bare bulb overhead. "Dust, thou art a scourge. Well, they don't call me 'Neet' for nothing." She pulled a clean rag from her pocket and wiped, reading as she went. "Intriguing titles: *Magyk Spells, Demonology, Occult Rituals, and Deadly Secrets.*"

She flipped open *Demonology.* The eyes of a fiend with dripping claws and fangs glinted from the illuminated frontispiece. "Ugh! Back into the box with you! *Magyk Spells,* this doesn't seem so scary."

Colourful illustrations of twisted plants and mushrooms accompanied incantations invoking long-forgotten gods. "What a crock!" she muttered. "But the pictures are pretty. What does that say?" She whispered the words, *"Acquire the blood of an unbaptized child and…"* Cold air slithered over her skin. She tossed the book into the crate. "That's enough of that. Anyway, I should hurry. Bingo starts at seven thirty."

When she arrived home, her brother called from the kitchen, "You're late. There's lasagna in the oven. The boys and I already had ours. They're upstairs playing."

"Smells delicious, John." Anita strolled into the kitchen to find him covered in tomato sauce and shaking peppercorns from his slippers. "I'll just grab a bite and head to bingo."

As she ate, she watched John scrub pots and fuss around the room. When he paused to admire his handiwork, Anita remarked, "Don't stop now, chef. You missed something." She pointed upwards, "There are tomato seeds on the ceiling. Man, you must be the messiest cook in the world, but you *are* the best." She hugged him and hurried upstairs to change, laughing, "By the way, there's a mushroom in your hair."

On her way down the hall, she stuck her head into the twins' bedroom, "I have to go out now, so… What are you little devils doing?"

Evander ran to the door. "Mama! We found pirate treasure in the closet!" A large wooden chest occupied the middle of the room. "Can we see?"

"Not tonight, my love. Maybe tomorrow. Now, be good for Uncle John." Anita pushed the box into the closet and closed the door.

***

IN THE SMOKY HAZE OF THE CHURCH HALL, Anita stood, unobserved, listening to the prattling bingo hawks.

"Huh!" Ruby scoffed. "That Anita Delaynie, she's so smug with her perfect children, her fancy clothes and that husband, always gone sailing around the world."

"I wish I had a husband like that." Shirley sighed. "My Alf is always there, every time I turn around. Imagine if he went away for months at a time and came back with gifts from India, China and who knows where."

"Who would do all your housework? Certainly not you, Shirley, you lazy thing. Anyway, at least you don't go teetering around in high heels, dressed up to the nines just to go to Bingo."

"Well, she doesn't go to church anymore, so where else is she going to flaunt her finery?"

Daphne Brown leaned close to Ruby and whispered. "I wonder what happens to the heathens when they die. Do you think there's a garden of heathen?"

Ruby ignored this weighty observance and blathered on, "Well, I know for a fact that Sally was devastated when her precious Anita went and married that Delaynie fella, him not belonging to any church or anything. Now, Sally never said anything, mind, but I can read people like a book and I know that marriage broke her heart. What kind of name is Sylvanius Delaynius anyway? Something pagan, no doubt. And those poor little boys, they don't even go to Sunday school with the rest of the youngsters. Now, if they were *my* grandchildren, I'd put my foot down, I tell you."

Anita slipped into her seat at the adjacent table. "Lovely evening, um, ladies. Are you talking about me and mine again? Well, you'd only be backbiting some other poor soul, I guess. By the way, Ruby, Delaynie is French. It means from the alder grove and Sylvanus was the Roman god of the forests." She lit a cigarette and smiled, turning her back on them. "If you need to know anything else, you're always welcome to come to the library and worship at the altar of erudition."

Ruby raised her voice, "So? She thinks she's an expert on everything, just because she works in a liberry. All that fancy talk don't impress me. Sounds like a load of gibberish."

Anita set out her bingo cards, ashtray and lucky charm. "Gladys isn't here yet?" She exhaled a lazy stream of smoke.

"Nope. She's usually the first one here," Shirley remarked.

"That's a lovely dress, Neet." Daphne sighed. "A present from your husband? What is it? Silk?"

Ruby ran her eye over Anita's elegant frame. "Huh! It can't be real though; real silk costs $50 a yard!"

"Well, Ruby, I don't buy my clothes by the yard." Anita laughed. "Oh, there's Gladys. Over here, Glad." She waved to attract her sister's attention.

Gladys nudged her way through the room and squeezed in beside Anita. "Good. You got our lucky table. Budge up. I can barely fit. Wow! Nice dress and new pearls, too. Sylvanus is back, I s'pose. He's the only man I know who can get his hands on black pearls."

"He's not back yet. His ship is a few days late. The kids are asking me every day, 'When is Daddy coming? Is he bringing presents?' They just can't wait for him to come home."

"I bet you can't wait either. Like a second honeymoon, what?" Gladys winked. "Anyway, I brought you a fresh dabber. It's not as elegant as pearls, but it's your lucky colour. "

"Thanks," Anita laughed and tapped the bright blue marker three times against the silver Bastet figurine. "I never win anyway, but we all have our little superstitions. Speaking of which, someone dropped off some old books for me at the library. I don't know who sent them, but they're really spoooooky. All about the occult and magic. Black magic! Ooooooh!"

"You shouldn't fool around with that stuff, Neet!" Gladys frowned. "For God's sake, don't let Mom catch wind of that. Remember the time she caught us with that Ouija board?"

"Yeah, she snapped it across her knee and tossed it in the wood stove, and do you remember what she said then?"

Gladys and Anita chorused together as they remembered their mother's next words, "We don't play board games with Satan in this house!"

Anita laughed. "But we're all grown up now; we can play with whomever we want."

Ruby jabbed Shirley's ribs with an elbow, "Hear that? Igrunt heathen!"

"I think Ruby just called me an ignorant heathen, Glad." Anita laughed again. "I should ask her to pray for my soul, no?"

"Who cares what she thinks? She's just a jealous old cow." Gladys crossed her fingers and clutched her lucky pendant, "Anyway, I hope one of us wins next month's jackpot! Five thousand dollars!"

"Huh!" Ruby puffed her cigarette and scowled. "God knows Anita doesn't need it. Or you either, Gladys. I hope someone deserving wins it. Now shush, Mr. Blair is getting ready to call the numbers."

"Someone deserving my eye! I hope that old dragon doesn't win," Gladys muttered to Anita. "But she wins something every week. *Lucky* old dragon!"

"I'd give *anything* to see the look on her face if one of *us* won it!"

"Shush!" Ruby glared.

For the rest of the evening, as Mr. Blair droned the numbers, Anita's thoughts wandered to the mysterious books with their bizarre illustrations. *Maybe I'll just go in tomorrow and finish unpacking.*

"BINGO!" Gladys jumped from her seat and waved her card.

"Huh! That's fifty dollars." Ruby scowled. "Last game of the night, too."

"But, Ruby, you won a hundred tonight, so what's your problem?" Shirley said.

***

EARLY SUNDAY MORNING, ANITA WOKE with Caspian's tiny fingers tugging

122

at her eyelids.

"Mama's awake! Show us the treasure!" he bounced onto the bed and Evander clambered up beside him.

"Up, Mama, up!" They chanted, "Up! Up!"

Anita slid from the bed into her slippers and robe. "Okay, you little pests. But aren't you hungry? I'm starved."

After breakfast, the boys led their mother to the bedroom and dragged the 'treasure' from the closet. The morning sun glanced off the chest, highlighting the gold crosses and silver doves that adorned the surface. Anita traced the designs with her finger. *I forgot how beautiful this was.*

"Open it, Mama," the boys begged. "Open it!"

She took a gold key from the dresser drawer and unlocked the chest. The children dove headfirst after their 'treasure.'

"Gently, boys. Sit quietly and I'll show you."

Anita found a small prayer book encased in mother of pearl with gold lettering.

"So pretty, Mama! Oh, beads!" Caspian grasped a handful of natural pearl rosaries; a gold crucifix glinted from each.

"Yes, they're pretty, but we don't want to break them." Anita untangled the strands and arranged them in their silk lined case.

"Help!" Evander dug into the chest wrestling with something heavy. Anita removed the boy and plopped him onto the floor. She pulled a large wooden crucifix from the chest. "I forgot about this, too." As she slid the gold icon forward, the rood opened to reveal several small bottles and a handwritten note, *To Anita, with all my love on your wedding day, Mom.*

"*Heathen!*" The word leaped into Anita's mind. She shut the box and pushed it into the closet. "I have to go out for a little while, my duckies.

Would you like to visit Nana Sally today? I'll ask Uncle John to take you."

"Yay!" The boys rushed downstairs.

When Anita reached the library steps, a group of neighbors were passing on their way home from church. Shirley, Daphne, and Ruby were among them. Shirley waved and called, "Hiya, Neet. Beautiful morning!"

Ruby scowled and Anita caught the words "Liberry... Sunday." Shirley blushed, but Daphne gave a little wave that escaped Ruby's notice.

Anita shrugged. "Have a nice day, folks!"

In the library cellar, with the bare bulb swinging overhead, Anita scanned the dust-covered crates and furniture huddled against the walls.

"I can put the books on those empty shelves at the back wall." She cleared off a desk, dragged the crate beside it and pulled up a chair. One by one, she removed the books and scanned the titles.

"*Everyday Potions and Spells.* Looks like a recipe book. Let's see: *How to Silence a Flibbertigibbet --* Gather wild mushrooms at midnight; add a personal item belonging to the gossip with a splash of bog water, let sit for three days... Say some magic words, and voila! *Bury at night near the prattler's house, guaranteed to shut its mouth.* Poetic, no? *Attract Abundance and Wealth -- Wrap three copper coins in white cotton, bury beneath an oak tree, mark the tree with a triple X --* say some more magic words and instant wealth! Easy peasy! *Protection from Evil –* Salt, silver, holy water, white crystals – the usual stuff."

She examined the entries, smiling at the archaic language and drawings. "I wonder if any of this stuff works. Maybe I'll try the money spell and win that five thousand. Glad will be glad. Ruby will be mad! Ha!" Anita took a notepad from her purse and wrote out the spell then glanced at her watch. "Three o'clock! I'd better get busy." For the next two hours, she swept, dusted and rearranged the cellar. Then she piled the books on the shelves along the wall. "They're not in any real order, but I'll organize them some other time."

She rushed home, fed and bathed the twins, then pulled out the notepad and went in search of three coppers. "It says I have to make a cotton bag from my own clothing." In the bedroom closet, she found an old shirt. "Perfect."

Just at sunset, Anita called to John, "I have to go outside for a minute. Put the kettle on, would you? I could murder a cup of tea."

He stood at the kitchen window and watched Anita run to the oak tree at the back of the garden. She dug a hole, dropped something in and read from a piece of paper while scraping the tree with a nail.

"I wonder what she's up to. Funny time of day for gardening! Oh, well, it's none of my business." He filled the kettle and put it on the stove.

**

EVERY EVENING FOR THE NEXT TWO WEEKS, once the library had closed, Anita would lock the door and head to the cellar where she examined the bizarre engravings and read the incantations aloud. She relished the sound of the archaic language flowing over her tongue like poetry. *Funny,* she thought, *it's not so scary anymore, and some of these pictures are beautiful.* She picked up a large leather-bound edition and admired its elaborate illustrations. *I should get them appraised, I suppose. Some collectors pay a fortune for these old things!*

Two weeks later, Anita and Gladys met at the church hall and settled at their lucky table to play for the jackpot. Anita's hands trembled as she laid out her Bingo cards and ashtray. She noticed Gladys watching and made an effort to steady herself as she lit a cigarette, but she dropped the lighter, knocking her Bastet figurine to the floor.

"What's with you? Are you worried about Sylvanus?" Gladys passed her the lighter and lucky charm.

"Of course I'm worried. I haven't heard a word from him."

"Well, maybe one of us will win that five thousand. That sure is a lot of money."

Anita thought, *then I'll know if there's anything to this magic spell business, too.* She said, "That would be great, Glad."

"Huh! Some people! The more they get, the more they want. Pure greed I calls it." Ruby addressed her tablemates, keeping her back to Gladys and Anita. "The husband ain't back yet? Typical sea-going type. Handsome fella like that, probly got a woman in every port. He probly got a whole family in every port, I dare say. It must get expensive, though when you have to get presents for every wife and every youngster. Expensive being so expansive." Ruby elbowed her friend. "Pretty clever, what? Mrs. Sylvanus Delaynie is not the only one who can string words together. What do you think, Shirley?" She lit a cigarette and released a cloud of blue smoke.

"Get you, with your fancy talk, but I think your big gob is going to get you into trouble one of these days, Ruby. That's what I think. You shouldn't go around bad-mouthing folks like that."

"I just tells it like it is." Ruby glowered at Shirley's audacity. Not that she knew it was called audacity, but she glowered all the same.

Daphne spoke up, "How do you know how it is? Neet's a lovely person with a lovely family. You're just jealous, Ruby. That's what I think."

Anita leaned back and laughed. "It looks like Daphne and Shirley finally got themselves a couple of backbones. Welcome to the phylum Chordata, ladies."

"Huh! Listen to herself over there!" Ruby huffed through her nostrils.

"Let it go, Ruby. Anyway, Mr. Blair is getting ready to call the numbers."

As the evening wore on and the jackpot game grew closer, excitement swelled the room. Ruby won a hundred dollars, Shirley and Daphne each won fifty.

I wonder if my experiment will work, Anita thought. She turned to her sister. "One of us is going to win that jackpot. I can just feel it."

"Now, ladies and gentlemen! Kiss your lucky charms and get your dabbers ready! Tonight, we're playing for our biggest jackpot ever. Five thousand smackeroos! Five thousand simoleans! Five thousand bucks! Five thousand big ones!"

"Oh, get on with it, you old windbag!" someone called from the back of the room. "Yeah, get on with it," everyone agreed.

"Okay, folks, here goes." Mr. Blair grew serious and all eyes watched the turning of the sacred drum as it mixed the bouncing balls. No one dared speak, cough or sneeze. No one dared disturb the sombre ceremony. "Our first number. B6, under the B, 6."

Anita nudged her sister, "Niacin. Like the vitamin. Hey, Glad, have a look at Ruby's tongue and see if she's getting enough B6!" They both laughed.

"There's nothing wrong with her tongue. It gets plenty of exercise! Maybe not enough fresh air, though."

"Quiet, you two," Ruby glared.

"Under the O, 69. O69. Keep the veiled remarks to yourselves, ladies and gents."

"Neet, ask Ruby if she knows what that means." Glad's comment drew black looks from the neighbouring table. The sisters burst into a fit of giggles.

Mr. Blair raised his eyebrows. "Ladies, when you have quite finished, I will continue." After Anita and Gladys simmered down, he called a string of numbers, pausing between each for dramatic effect.

When he called out B9, Anita blurted out, "Like that useless lump on Ruby's neck! Get it? B9! Wha – ha –ha ha ! Benign!"

Gladys grabbed Anita's arm. "You're on the hitch! You just need one more number for the jackpot!"

Anita gritted her teeth. "Come on, O66!"

Ruby hissed, "That witch is on the hitch!"

Mr. Blair took a deep breath. "I can feel the excitement, folks. We just have a few more left in the drum and the next number is... is everybody listening? O66! Under the O, 66!"

Gladys jumped from her seat, "BINGO! Neet you got it! You got Bingo. Neet, what's wrong? You won!"

A wasp nest droned in Anita's ears and the room spun. *It worked! The money spell worked! Was it just a coincidence?*

A shrill voice pierced Anita's brain, "She doesn't deserve it! That heathen coming into our nice game and winning it all! It shouldn't be allowed!" Ruby waddled to the stage where Mr. Blair stood agape.

"Please go back to your seat, Mrs. Button. We have to verify Mrs. Delaynie's numbers. Bill, are you there?" Mr. Blair searched the crowd for assistance. "Oh, there you are."

Big Bill McTavish guided Ruby to her table. "Calm down, now Missus. There's no need for you to be getting on like that."

"Huh!" Ruby dropped into her seat and lit a cigarette. "The nerve!"

"Now, Mrs. Delaynie, please pass your card to Bill so we can check your numbers."

Anita's fingers trembled as she handed over her card. Mr. Blair and Bill checked the numbers aloud.

"Well folks, it looks like we have a winner! Mrs. Delaynie, you may come to my office on Monday morning to claim your prize. Congratulations!"

"What will you do with all that money, Neet?"

"I don't know, sis. Maybe I'll buy a diamond ring or a new car." She turned to face the neighbouring table. "Or maybe I'll give it all away!"

"Well! Of all the!" Ruby slammed the table. An ashtray crashed to the floor, flinging glass in every direction. Anita spied something silver among the shards near Ruby's whale-blubber feet.

"You're upsetting yourself, Ruby. Let's get you home." Shirley and Daphne each took one of their friend's arms and led her from the hall.

Anita retrieved the small silver object. *Ruby's lucky four-leaf clover. How fortuitous!* She slipped it into her pocket. "Come on, Glad. Let's go. That was fun, but I can't take any more excitement."

***

WHEN ANITA GOT HOME, SHE PEEKED into the boys' room. Four bright eyes gleamed in the darkness.

"Evander, why aren't you asleep? Why are you so tense, Kitty?" She reached to pet the large grey cat coiled like a spring on the foot of the bed.

"Mama, come here," the boy whispered. "There's a man up there." He pointed to the ceiling over his bed. The cat growled. "Kitty and me, we don't like him, Mama."

She wrapped his small body in her arms. "Oh, honey, you must have been dreaming."

"No, Mama. He's still there. He's talking to me."

"What's the man saying?

Evander put a finger to his lips. "Sh, he says, sh."

Kitty hissed and sprang from the bed. Anita hugged her son and directed an angry stare toward the ceiling. *"Stay away from my children!"*

Anita sat with Evander until she felt him relax in her arms. She glanced at her watch. *Almost midnight.*

***

AT THE EDGE OF THE GARDEN, the forest loomed, dark and sweet smelling. Her pocket flashlight clicked. The wavering beam lit her path through the woods. Something white started from the darkness. *A fairy ring. That's convenient, right next to the bog.* Keeping an eye on her watch, she waited until the hands ticked over to midnight, then she gathered wild mushrooms and filled a bottle from the bog. "Now, let's see if this magic spell stuff is for real."

***

ON SUNDAY MORNING, ANITA GOT UP EARLY, headed for the library cellar with her supplies, and found the 'Flibbertigibbet spell.' *I wonder if this will seal Ruby's nasty lips.*

On a desk in the corner, she dumped the mushrooms, bog water and Ruby's four-leaf clover into a copper pot, covering it with a cotton cloth. She waved her hands over the pot and read the incantation aloud. The library floor creaked above her head and the bare lightbulb shed a wavering circle of light. Something scratched and slithered inside the wall. Anita choked. *Mice.*

Three nights later, she returned to the cellar and chanted another incantation over the copper pot. She emerged from the library and hurried along the road clutching a small wrapped bundle. "Bury at night near the gossip's house, guaranteed to shut its mouth." She whispered the enchanted words aloud as she hurried along the road until she came to a small grey cottage. Ruby leaned out the window smoking a cigarette.

Anita held her breath and stood motionless by the garden gate. *I wonder*

130

if she can see me. She lifted her hand and waved. Ruby doused her cigarette and turned from the window. Anita slipped through the gate into the shadows where she dug a hole in the loose garden loam.

"Into the hole you go!" She dropped the package and whispered the vital words then ducked from the garden and scurried down the dark road. *Magic test number two... check!*

***

TWO DAYS LATER, GLADYS CALLED ANITA AT THE LIBRARY. "Neet, we have to go to see Dr. Roberts right away! Ruby has come down with some strange disease and he wants to see everyone who has been in close contact. It may be contagious!"

Anita smiled into the phone, "Oh, really? What's she got? Something wrong with her scurrilous mouth?"

"How - how did you know? When she talks, it comes out all gibberish. Come on, Neet. Tell Mr. Page you have to go and see the doctor right away."

"I can't leave. There's no one else here. Come down and we can talk about it. Besides, I want to show you something."

Gladys rushed into the library and found Anita perched behind the desk, flipping through a fashion magazine. "How pretty! This yellow dress would look lovely with my black pearls."

"Neet, please come with me to see Dr. Roberts. Ruby is sick and everyone's worried. What if you or your boys catch it, whatever it is?" Gladys leaned over the desk and tugged at the magazine. "Sylvanus will be home soon. You don't want him to find you ill."

Anita patted her sister's hand, "Oh, calm down, Silly. We'll be fine." She stood and led Gladys to the cellar door. "Now, come with me. I have to show you something. It's my little secret."

She unlocked the door and led the way down, flicking the wall switch. Yellow light swung across the cellar floor, illuminating intricate symbols scratched into the cement.

"What is all this, Neet? What have you been doing down here?" Gladys stared at the patterns that seemed to move on their own. Anita drifted around the room, lighting candles and whispering.

Then, she grasped Glad's hand and dragged her to the bookshelf. She chose a mouldy tome and flipped it open. "Here. Read this."

Glad's eyes widened. "Are you – are you telling me you think this has something to do with Ruby? Is she the flibbertigibbet?" She let the book fall.

Anita laughed. "I shut her nasty gob, that's all. We can go to bingo and not have to listen to her slagging us off. Not only that, we're going to win again. Look." She flipped the pages to show the money spell.

"But Neet, you don't believe this stuff, do you? It's just a coincidence about the jackpot and Ruby."

"I like to win and knowing that it gets on her nerves, well, that's just a bonus, now isn't it?" Anita's eyes gleamed and shadows moved under the delicate skin.

Gladys shivered. "Come home, Neet. Come home and see your boys. When does Sylvanus get back?"

Anita shook her head and tears glinted in the yellow light. "I haven't heard from him. The shipping company has no news, either." She bit her lip, dragged another book from the shelf, and scanned the pages. "Do you think I can find a spell to bring a missing husband home?" The patterns on the floor swam before her eyes. "Here's one for protection. Maybe not."

"No more spells. He'll be back soon. Please promise me, Neet, no more of this foolishness. You're making yourself ill."

"Okay. No more spells." She added in a whisper, "for now."

***

ANITA TRIED TO KEEP HER PROMISE AND STAY AWAY from the library cellar, but on Friday afternoon, she hesitated near the door with the key in her hand.

Maybe if I lock it, I won't be tempted. The key clicked into place and a low mocking laugh echoed in her ears. She smacked the door with her open hand. "Leave me alone!"

"What's the trouble, Anita? Are you okay?" Turner called from behind the desk.

"Sorry, I'm not feeling well. I think I'll leave early today."

He waved his hand. "Sure, sure. Go. Bill and I can close up."

When Anita arrived home, John had just hung up the telephone.

"Great news, Neet! That was the manager of the shipping company. Syl will be home next Thursday. Apparently, the crew became ill and they had to quarantine in some remote port. Word just came today that they're on their way back."

Anita steadied herself against the doorjamb. Tears filled her eyes. "Finally!"

"Mama! Mama! Is Daddy coming home?" Caspian and Evander ran to her and each grabbed a leg.

She hugged them to her. "Yes, my darlings!"

"Is that because we prayed to Almighty God?" Evander asked.

Anita snapped, "Who prayed?"

"Nana Sally said we should pray for Daddy because you were too busy, but somebody had to do it and..."

"It's a secret, Vander," Caspian whispered.

133

"But Nana said it would be okay to think happy thoughts for Daddy." Evander started to cry. "Please don't be mad, Mama!"

"I'm sorry. I'm not angry, my ducky. I was worried, too. But your happy thoughts worked." Anita knelt and kissed his wet face. "Why don't you two sleep with me in the big bed tonight?"

***

ANITA AWOKE AT DAYBREAK, slipped from the house and headed to the library. She dragged a box of cleaning supplies to the cellar and scoured the floor with a wire brush. "There, gone. For good."

"Now, to get rid of these." She picked up *Demonology* and tossed it into the crate. "Ugh! Something's burning!" She sniffed, "But, I didn't light any candles." Heavy blue-grey smoke poured in through a fissure in the cellar wall. The greasy vapour swirled upward, building itself into a solid mass. The floor overhead groaned, and the bare bulb swung wildly. Anita dropped to her knees.

"The things! The floor! It's all back! But I scrubbed it!" Her heart twitched wildly, and she clawed at the floor shredding her fingernails. Grinning faces filled the room and voices jeered and buzzed in her skull. The cellar door slammed.

***

ANITA ARRIVED AT THE CHURCH HALL and slid into her usual seat.

"Why didn't you tell me you had heard from Sylvanus? John says he's coming home in a few days. You must be relieved." Gladys reached for Anita's hand, but she jerked it away and fumbled in her purse for cigarettes.

"I didn't hear from him. The shipping company phoned."

"Well, same difference. Anyway, you don't seem best pleased and you look ill."

"Of course I'm pleased."

"Well, tell that to your face."

"I was sick. Sick with worry, you know that. And... and... something happened tonight. You'll think I'm half cracked, but I have to tell someone, and you're the only one I can trust."

"So, come on, spill." Gladys leaned closer and stared into Anita's wild eyes.

"It's too crowded and noisy here. Come outside, would you?"

"Can it wait until after bingo? It should be good tonight without Ruby and her clique. I know I said I feel sorry for her, but... Well, look who's waddling this way." Gladys nodded toward the door where Ruby had just entered supported by Shirley and Daphne. "You wouldn't expect her to go out in public."

"She looks like she's been pulled through a knothole. Her hair is like a birch broom in the fits."

Ruby and Daphne took their seats, but Shirley disappeared beneath the table. "I'll have a look, but it won't be here. They clean this place every day. It probably went in the garbage with the broken glass."

Ruby uttered some gibberish and Daphne translated. "Glad, you didn't happen to see Ruby's silver good luck charm, did you? It's a four-leaf clover pendant."

Anita smiled. "What's the matter, Mrs. Button? Can't speak for yourself?"

Ruby's face flamed. "A din blick thone do doe."

Shirley translated, "She's been sick, don't you know? Show them your tongue."

"Ahh!" Ruby obliged and out flopped a scaly appendage. A pool of green saliva slopped onto the table. A crowd gathered to stare, cluck their tongues, and offer sympathy and handkerchiefs.

"Gross!" Anita whispered as she turned her back and rooted through her handbag. *Serves her right.* She smiled and passed Ruby a handkerchief.

Daphne mopped the table. "The poor thing. Dr. Roberts says he's never seen anything like it. Maybe it's allergies. Anyway, it doesn't seem to be contagious, thank God. Ruby thinks it's because she lost her good luck charm."

Anita turned away and stifled a giggle. Gladys prodded her under the table.

"It's not funny. Don't you feel bad for her?"

"I think she's enjoying the attention. She's never been so popular!"

More gibberish flowed from the neighbouring table. Ruby shook her wild red head and scowled at Anita as Daphne translated, "She wants to know why you're laughing at her."

Ruby sputtered, "By do do thate thee tho?"

Anita lost control. "What – ha- ha – what did she say? Fe fie foe fum?"

"She wants to know why you hate her so."

"Well, why don't you try to figure that out... Oh, forget it! Let's go, Glad." Anita turned blazing eyes on Ruby's entourage. "Thanks for the entertainment, but I'm no longer in the mood." She pushed through the gaping crowd and stalked out into the night, followed by Gladys.

Anita grabbed her sister's arm and pulled her into the shadow of the building. "Glad, I need to tell you something. It's really important."

"Well, I know one thing, you're definitely not yourself. I thought you would feel a little sorry for Ruby. Teasing someone is one thing, but even that ignorant old battle axe doesn't deserve to be ridiculed when she's ill."

"I did feel a little bad at first, but tonight when I saw her, it just cracked me up. I had to get out of there before I took credit for it. They already think I'm some kind of barbarian. Anyway, I need to tell you about today in the library. I feel like everything is out of control because of those horrid spells, so I went back to the cellar to get rid of the marks on the floor and the books."

"Well, thank God!" Gladys sighed and leaned against the wall. "And when Sylvanus gets home, everything can go back to normal."

"No, Glad, it can't go back to normal. It's The Fallen, they want payment. They say they did my bidding, now I must do theirs. They want… I keep hearing the voices in my head."

"The what? The who? What voices?"

"I try to make it stop, but it's too late. There's nothing I can do. I thought if I got rid of the books, things would go back to normal. Today, while I was packing everything away, these things appeared. A demon straight out of that book with claws and scales and an enormous green dog-like beast with red eyes. They called themselves The Fallen and they said I must bring them an unbaptized child. They want one of my boys. Oh, Glad, I'm terrified!"

"But, Neet. That's nonsense. All that messing about in the cellar by yourself, well, it's just not healthy. Go home to your family and be thankful that Syl will be back soon." Gladys turned to leave. "Now, good night. I'll see you tomorrow, maybe."

When she had walked about a hundred yards, she glanced back to see Anita standing alone, staring into the shadows as if she were listening. Gladys shrugged and continued on her way.

***

ANITA *WAS* LISTENING, HER BODY bent toward the darkness. Listening to footsteps crunch on the gravel road. Someone whispered. It was a sigh like wind through beech leaves.

"Who's there?" she called. "Oh! Please, no!" Anita clamped her hands over her ears. The air buzzed and long shadows stretched toward her. Cold fingers tightened around her throat. Her brain screamed, *RUN!* She kicked off her stilettoes and rushed along the gravel road to the suspension bridge. It swayed beneath her and she stared into the swirling black water. Her own bloody footprints gleamed on the wooden planks.

Laughter echoed in the gloom. Anita shook her fist and screamed into the night, "YOU'RE NOT GETTING MY GODDAMN YOUNGSTERS!" Ignoring her damaged feet, she continued her mad dash toward home.

"They're coming, they're coming!" she gasped and panted as she tore into the cottage. The door slammed and she fell against it. John emerged from the kitchen, shaking clouds of flour from his hair.

"What's going on, Sis?"

"Don't open that door whatever you do. Where are the boys?"

"They're asleep."

"HURRY!" she yelled. "Get the box of salt from the kitchen!"

John froze staring into her panicked eyes.

"Oh, get out of my way and don't open that door!" She pushed him aside and ran for the kitchen.

He stood scratching his head staring at the bloody trail she left behind. Anita rushed from the kitchen tossing handfuls of rock salt across the floor throughout the entranceway and into the front parlour.

"Here take this." She passed him the salt. "Spread it on the floor near the doors and under all the windows. DON'T OPEN THAT DOOR!" She ran up the stairs.

Something scratched and growled on the walkway outside. It pounded on the front door, shaking the windowpanes and steaming the glass with its hot breath. A caustic smoke seeped into the front hall.

"Neet, someone's at the door." John called up the stairs.

"DON'T OPEN IT!"

He shrugged and strolled through the house, sprinkling the salt. "And she says I'm messy!"

Upstairs in the boys' bedroom, Anita dragged the wooden chest from the closet. With trembling hands, she removed the large crucifix and slid it open to reveal the tiny bottles of oil and water. She grasped the bottles and read the notes.

"More magic spells and incantations." She chewed her lower lip until she tasted blood. The pounding downstairs grew louder, shaking the floor beneath her feet.

John called again, "Neet, someone's at the door!"

"DON'T OPEN THAT GODDAMN DOOR, JOHN!"

She performed the ritual detailed in her mother's notes, sprinkling holy water and anointing each of the sleeping children with sacred oil. "Evander Delaynie, I baptise thee… Caspian Delaynie, I baptise thee."

The pounding echoed through the cottage rattling the glass in the windows. Anita knelt on the floor with her hands over her ears. "Please make it stop. Please!"

A shadow passed across the room. She uncovered her ears and looked up to see John in the doorway.

"Didn't you hear me, Neet? I'm going to bed now. Good night."

Silence echoed through the house. She sat by the bed, gazing at her sleeping children. "They didn't even know…"

***

Four days later, Sylvanus Delaynie walked into a silent house. "Hello! Where is everybody?"

Sally appeared from the kitchen, wringing her hands. "Sylvanus, you better sit down." She took his hand and led him to the parlour.

"Where are Anita and the children? A fine welcome this is, I don't think! A man is gone for months and comes home to..." He noticed her red swollen eyes. "What is it? What's wrong?" He sat on the sofa and lowered his voice. "Is it bad news?"

Sally sat next to him and took his hand. "The boys are with Gladys at her house. They're fine, but Anita has been missing since Saturday night. John says she came home scared out of her wits, claiming someone was following her, but he couldn't see anything outside and Anita told him not to open the door. John said he left her in the boys' room and went to bed. The next morning, she was gone. We've searched everywhere: the woods, the library, the hospitals and... everywhere."

***

THE NEXT DAY, GLADYS SHOWED UP AT THE LIBRARY. "Mr. Page, I believe Anita left some personal belongings, you know, books and stuff."

"We have her things packed up and Bill thought he would just drop them off to save you the trouble. I think we have everything."

"Do you mind if I check the cellar? I think she may have left some things and I'd like to have them, if you don't mind or maybe she left a clue..."

"Sure, no problem. We rarely go down there anyway." He tossed her the key. "I found this on the desk."

Gladys flicked the light switch and crept down the stairs, expecting to find the images on the floor, the burnt candles and the mouldy books. Discarded furniture, empty crates and shelves cluttered the space.

140

Something glinted in the dust and she stooped to retrieve it. Tears filled her eyes and she dropped the silver Bastet figurine into her pocket. "I'm sorry, Neet."

The next morning, Bill found a large envelope on the library steps. The label read *T. Page c/o Lance Cove Library*. He glanced up and down the empty street.

"Package for you, Turner." Bill dropped the envelope onto the desk.

Turner opened the package and read the printed note. *Dear Turner: I know you will put this to good use. Give it to an orphanage or an old folks' home. You could even buy some books or give it to the church.*

He counted out the pile of bills.

Bill whistled. "Wow! Five grand!"

***

SYLVANUS LINGERED IN THE DOORWAY of his empty bedroom. He hadn't slept for... how long? "What day is it? Has it really been a month?"

From down the hall, he heard a faint whimper, like a small animal in distress. He crept to the boys' bedroom. A pair of bright eyes gleamed in the darkness and a small voice whispered, "Daddy, come here."

"Cas? What is it? Why are you still awake? Everyone else is asleep, even Kitty." He stroked the cat's warm fur. She butted her head against his hand and rumbled.

"Daddy, there's a lady up there." Caspian pointed to the ceiling.

"Oh, Buddy, you must have been dreaming." Sylvanus wrapped his arms around the small shoulders.

"No, Daddy. She's still there. She's talking to me."

"What's she saying, Bud?"

Caspian placed a finger against his lips. "Sh, she says, sh."

Regnum

By Wanying Zhang

MAY LI

"When are you going to get married?" my mother asks for what feels like the thousandth time.

I let out an audible sigh of frustration as my patience wears thinner than I thought possible.

"Mom, I'm just not ready. I haven't found anyone interesting."

"See what happens when you lazy?"

"Mom, just give it a rest! I just got back from work, I have other things to do."

"Oh, like what? Sleeping? You certainly not see your family enough!"

"Look, I need to wrap up some stuff for work. I'll talk to you later!"

"Work? You care about work now, suddenly? Your uncle Jinglong gives you work, takes care of you. You should attend his family gatherings and thank him more!"

"Whatever, mom. I have to go now."

"Ay, don't forget to eat dinner!"

I hang up the phone, walk into my bedroom and crash onto the mattress. Barely a minute passes before my phone vibrates again. I look at it to see my uncle's name lighting up the screen. I let out a low groan.

***

JINGLONG LI

She has to listen to me this time; it's for her own good. I swipe my iPhone and dial May's number. No response on the first try. I ring again. She picks up this time on the third ring.

"May, I haven't seen you since last week! What have you been up to?"

"Oh, you know, the usual. Working and stuff." She's hiding something; I can sense it in her tone. I should pacify her.

"Good, good. Listen, we're having dinner tomorrow with some family friends, you must join us."

"I don't know…" She thinks she's in control again.

"I won't take no for an answer. Why don't you take tomorrow off to get ready? I will send you the money for a new dress and shoes." She loves shopping and hates work, she will take the bait.

"But I…"

"No buts. See you tomorrow at 7 pm. Don't be late and look sharp."

***

MAY LI

"Ugh! I hate my job. I wish I didn't have to work at my uncle's stupid company," I almost yell to Amber and Tanya over the din of lunch-time conversation at the Regnum cafeteria. The pane glass windows do nothing to dispel the sense of claustrophobia that continuously haunts the facility.

"What would you rather do instead?" Amber asks me. She is the new girl at work, just moved into town, and in her early twenties. A shy, but bright eyed girl and she is eager to please. She always seems to be working, keeping herself busy probably trying to prove herself. Newly wedded to her husband back in India, she certainly does talk about him a lot.

"I don't know. I kind of regret studying sciences sometimes... I let my uncle talk me into it 'cause it has a more secure future.' Now I'm stuck in this hellhole with nowhere else to go."

"Well, at least we have benefits," Tanya says, grinning around a mouthful of pad thai. She is a single mother of three, emigrated from Nigeria. Only in her early thirties, but dark circles tarnish her once beautiful eyes and her body constantly slouches forward. Her dark hair pulled back in a simple bun which barely contains loose fragments dangling forward as she eats.

"And, hey, it's nice contributing to the scientific community. I mean Regnum is doing some pretty cool stuff in drug discovery and some of the work we do is pretty exciting!" Amber pitches in.

I start wondering how these two manage to invest in the daily grind so fully. They must be the 'real, honest workers' that my uncle is so fond of.

"It'd be even more exciting if we got paid better though. And the machines didn't break down every few days," Tanya adds sardonically.

"I guess. But you still haven't told us what you'd rather do instead,

May," Amber inquires.

"Maybe I could travel for a bit? I feel so trapped here. Maybe I need a change of scenery. I have always wanted to see Japan or England. Possibly even New Zealand," I reply dourly.

"You're so lucky you can think about traveling. I don't think I can travel for at least another five years," Tanya contemplates in dismay.

"Oh, why is that?"

"Well the children are too young, and I simply can't afford it. I can't even afford to go back to my country to visit. I'm trying to hold down a second job as well."

I suppose people who have children have no lives. That's why I have three cats instead.

"Yeah traveling the world does sound lovely. But my husband and I should probably save up some money first," Amber chimes in.

"But you're young, you should travel," I say to Amber.

"I'm sure we'll get the chance someday."

She probably won't get around to it. She barely spent any money on her honeymoon.

"Actually, we did travel around India a bit when we first got married..." Amber continues. But I quickly lose interest in the conversation. My mind eventually wanders to this guy I recently met through online dating.

Naturally, my uncle and my family don't know about him. We have been on a few dates and I thought we had a connection, but he seems to be ghosting me lately. Or maybe he's just busy. I just can't seem to get this romance thing right. I've been trying online dating for a while, but all the men are uninteresting and I can't bring myself to tell any of them about my crazy family.

***

I didn't take the entire day off after all as my uncle suggested, but I did take half a day off to go shopping. I don't think people will miss me. I message Amber.

>Time to go to another one of these dinners. 🙁

>Try to have fun.

She messages back. She doesn't get it. I have to sit through these dinners every week. Sometimes two or three times a week depending on my uncle's whim.

>It's going to be torture…

>Well at least it's free food.

She's totally missing the point. I'd rather go on food stamps than go to these elaborate dinners with my uncle. But I have to please him. And my mother will ask me afterwards how it went and make me go over every detail.

***

JINGLONG LI

Everything must go as planned today. The Chens arrive at 6:00 pm sharp as I anticipate. I flew them in from Hangzhou, of course; I must let them know I have the upper hand. I open the door to find Chen Tianbao flanked by his beaming parents. I welcome them into my condo unit which, thanks to a pair of cleaners I hired the week before, was spotless tonight. After a brief, but cordial exchange of greetings, we move to the kitchen to enjoy caviar tartlets and sparkling wine.

I met Tianbao's father, Wei, a few years earlier on one of my many business trips to China. Back then, Wei had been the owner of a small business supplying parts to telecom equipment manufacturers. His success had been far from assured but I had an intuition that Wei would outcompete other shops doing the same thing. Indeed, Wei was now the head of a thriving company employing thousands of people across China. Much like myself, Wei had started with nothing but his entrepreneurial spirit and had built something for himself. Also like me, Wei has never forgotten his duty to his family and has provided many of his relatives with stable well-paid jobs. Although I doubt that he bestows generous benefits and bonuses like I do. Not to mention that I have personally intervened to set up some of my more wayward relatives with respectable spouses. A lot of them wouldn't even know what to do with themselves if it weren't for me, it's all for their own good. I really am a saint.

In fact, I am afraid I have to intervene once more and the Chens are here tonight to further that purpose. May has been very willful lately. Dangling money in front of her usually soothes her nerves, but if she doesn't get her life together soon, I fear that she will end up aimless and adrift. I think it is time that May learned the discipline and duty of family life. And there is no better start to a good family than a good husband.

Tianbao, or Tony as he likes to be called, is around my niece's age. Single, 35, reasonable six figure income, handsome enough. Plays golf in his spare time, very respectable, a dutiful reader of *The Economist*, graduated *summa cum laude* from Tsinghua University. A dependable Chinese man who would not even expect his wife to work for a living. Can't go wrong with that. I would even venture that he is too good for May. May cannot refuse the young man I have found for her this time; fellows like him only come around once in a generation. One day, she will appreciate all that I have done for her. I wish I had found someone like this for my own daughter, Mimi, but her untimely passing was deeply regrettable. I often see her in May; her fiery brown eyes, her mother and her aunt's full lips, always having something deplorable to say. They even wear their hair the same, always down, shoulder-length, with a slight curl at the ends. I used to like patting my daughter's head when she was younger since she had always been such an obedient daughter.

May, on the other hand, has some work to do in the manners department and she needs to be taught about respect. She is always having temper tantrums or going on about some gossip about her friends. She is often late, lazy and has questionable choices in her fashion. I have to tell her a hundred times to cover up more and not dress like a slut. I hope this time she will dress in something decent and respectable. Well, I blame her parents for not bringing her up right. When I received her, she was already damaged goods, so there is only so much I can do; but I will not give up on her. She is family after all.

***

May Li

I put on a floral cocktail dress that makes me look classy but casual. For my makeup, I apply some foundation to even out my complexion and bring out its natural glow. I finish off with some sheer lip gloss that highlights the fullness of my lips. I don't put much more effort though since it's probably going to be the usual crowd at my uncle's dinner tonight. That means some of my aunts, uncles, their kids and whatever hapless soul has decided to be my uncle's entertainer of the week. Like a herd of sheep, they gather at my uncle's dinner table to receive what he chooses to bestow on them. Gifts, jobs, trips abroad, tuition for their kids' private schools, funds for starter homes, the list goes on. A lot of the time, he'll arrange flights to or from China for our relatives. He practically treats them like cattle being transported across the globe. Recently, he's even thought of buying everyone gym memberships so they can all go get some exercise together or something.

But I know that it's all a façade. Really, he just wants people to worship him for his wealth and his success. I can't bring this up to them of course; my relatives would accuse me of being an entitled brat who should be grateful for her uncle's generosity. Instead, we let the conversation revolve around my uncle and the sort of family gossip he deems worthy of sharing: who's getting married to whom, or more importantly, the net worth and pedigree of the betrothed, how many kids does one have, which schools the kids are going to and so on. Occasionally, my uncle will bring up work but it's usually to talk about some co-worker who probably deserves to be let go due to their "lack of work ethic."

The worst, however, is when the conversation turns to me. There will be the usual questions about whether I have a man in my life, when I'll get around to learning how to drive, advice on where and at what price I should buy property for investment and how I shouldn't delay too long on having kids. Sometimes, I just get so pissed off that I want to turn over the dining table and spill expensive wine all over their fine clothing. But as my uncle always reminds me of my manners, most of the time I can divert my relatives' interest into critiquing my colleagues Amber and Tanya. Not that I care that much about their boring and tedious lives. But my relatives seem to have a lot of comments on how deep in debt Amber is, or about how Tanya should have planned out her pregnancies. They say things like, "Oh, she should have made better financial decisions about her future," or "Some cultures should learn that it's better to have fewer but smarter kids." On top of being obnoxious, my relatives are also casually racist.

In any case, given that my uncle sent me some money this time to upgrade my "worn down" and "inappropriate" wardrobe, maybe there are some special guests tonight that he wants to impress. At 6:55 pm, I ring the doorbell to my uncle's three bedroom condo. I make sure to stand up straight so that my uncle doesn't comment on my posture yet again. I also take care to show up five minutes early to avoid accusations of laziness. But I'm sure he'll find something else to criticize anyway. I spot his Tesla and Mercedes parked outside and, for a split second, I fantasize about jumping into one of them and taking off to Mexico. My uncle opens the door, beaming down on me, wearing a formal suit and tie. He seems to approve of my wardrobe choices tonight. A miasma of his Armani cologne wafts through the doorway as he gestures me in. He puts a hand on the small of my back to steer me and as a reminder to act appropriately.

The inside of his condo looks as new as the day he bought it. Not a speck of dust threatens the polished surfaces of the unit and air fresheners make the condo smell welcoming. There is a Roomba neatly tucked away in the corner, the appliances are sparkling clean and a decorative chandelier hangs from the ceiling scattering a kaleidoscope of glittering light around the living room. I enter the dining room, which faces his open kitchen. The solid wood Qing dining table is laid out with my uncle's bone china dinnerware. A family of three is seated around the circular dinner table.

"May, meet our guests, Chen Tianbao and his parents," Jinglong says. "They just flew in from China."

My eyes bulge and my mouth goes slack at the sight in front of me. My uncle presses his hand gently into my back. I press my lips together and try my best to maintain a polite smile. Jinglong gestures for me to pour some hot tea for our guests. I approach the table, pick up the fine teapot and start pouring tea while keeping my eyes lowered.

"Nice to meet you," I say quietly, trying to suppress a grimace.

I know exactly what this is. This is another set up for a dinner date with some guy my uncle has picked out for me. Tianbao sits across from me with a lopsided smile. His eyes peer out from his thick glasses pushed up against a bulbous nose. I feel him sizing me up like a prize-winning pig at the market as I pour him the tea. I can't tell if his black hair is arranged with gel or is just naturally greasy.

We quickly dig into a dinner of freshly made Sichuan pork, Chinese broccoli in oyster sauce and steaming rice. Ordinarily, I would eat these favorite dishes with gusto. But tonight, I can barely get through a few bites. Tianbao's parents sit solemnly across the table from me. I bet they are silently judging me while they eat. Tianbao's father is an older carbon copy of the son, down to the bulbous nose, the ugly glasses and the greasy hair. The mother is a plump creature with small beady eyes and cheeks painted with vivid red rouge that's wildly incongruous with expensive but tacky gold jewelry.

"This is very nice place you have," Tianbao's mother compliments my uncle.

"Oh this is nothing. You should see my place in Vancouver," Jinglong says.

"Where you invest in?"

"Locations where the rental market is favorable, of course. I have property in Toronto, Hong Kong and New York. Other than that, I have a small cottage in Malibu and a charming chalet in Vermont."

"Ah, I have properties in most of those places too!" Tianbao's father exclaims, "I want your advice on properties in Canada…"

I'm already bored of this conversation. As I play with my food, I ruefully think that Jinglong should let Tanya live in one of his properties. I've been to her place; it's a cramped run-down apartment with peeling yellow plaster, creaky wooden floors and dim lights hanging from the low ceiling. It is way too small to fit her three kids, the basement floods in the spring and the house is drafty in the winter. It would be better for her if she got a new place.

"Wonderful! I would love to visit some of those places sometime." Jinglong goes on.

"Of course, anytime! But we're here to talk about May and Tianbao," Tianbao's mother interjects.

My ears perk up at the sound of my name but I continue picking away at my pork and rice.

"So my son, ah very accomplished. Graduated top in his class at Tsinghua University. One of the youngest male to make tech start-up. How about you?" It takes me a second to realize that she directs the question at me. Here comes the brutal interview.

"I studied at, uh McGill and I'm a research scientist now."

"Ah good, good. What you plan to do after you marry? We expect you to still be able to perform wifely duties if you choose to continue work. But of course, our son will provide for you and make sure you have everything you need." I almost choke on my food at the question.

"Of course, she will be delighted to do both! She is very skilled at multitasking," Jinglong chimes in.

"You plan to have children?" the mother continues. When will this nightmare end?

**

"So what are your hobbies?" Tianbao tries asking. After an hour or so of keeping a flat conversation at the dinner table during which his parents bragged about their son and questioned my ambitions and goals in life, the others left us alone for us to "talk." I struggle to understand him through his thick accent. I tried speaking some Chinese, but that seemed to confuse him more. My brain already feels like jelly from all the questioning. Poor guy, I don't particularly care to get to know him. I just want him out of my life.

"Look, I don't want to do this." Confusion clouds his face, so I explain further. "They brought you here to pair us up, but I'm not interested. It's nothing to do with you, I just don't want to right now."

"Oh," he looks down at his hands.

"You don't want to get involved with our family. My uncle will just control everyone, including you."

"I don't understand."

"Let me guess, he probably gave you some incentive to come here right? What is it?"

"Well, he flew us here and promised to invest in my start-up," Tianbao says absently.

"See what I mean? He will always have control. Once you accept, he is going to manipulate you further. You won't be able to say no."

"I will try to be good to you. My parents want this for me too." He shifts uncomfortably. I almost feel sorry for him.

**

JINGLONG LI

"Why do you keep setting me up with these people? How many times do I have to tell you? I'm not interested!" May turns to me to protest as soon as the guests leave. I had anticipated that she would perhaps put up some resistance. Poor May, she just can't see what's good for her.

"I'm simply looking out for what is best for you. Look at you. You're thirty-four, no man, no future, you don't even exercise to try to make yourself look good. At least you have a job thanks to me! Now you dress a little better, eat a bit nicer."

"I have enough! I don't want your selection of men, or your money or whatever, just leave me alone." We always have this argument, but she will always come crawling back to me.

"See how long you can survive without me. Go on try to look for another job. You think it's that easy?"

"Why can't you just leave me alone?"

"Oh I wish I could, May. Your parents need support from me, or think of all the suffering they will have to endure. You know your mother has a bad back and your dad cannot afford a therapist on his own. They reached out to me, and I promised them to look out for you here, give you a better life. I paid for your education, gave you money to indulge yourself. Now I'm trying to make your life even better by finding you a good man. The least you can do is follow my advice." I know it hurts her whenever I play the parents card, but she leaves me no other choice. She must know her place. I continue.

"Remember when you wanted to move out from my condo and I wanted you to stay? You know it hurt me, but I let you have your independence. You were the only family I had when I first came to Canada. But you grew up so fast. Yet, I still helped you pick out a nice apartment, didn't I? I just want you to be nearby. You understand, May?"

Her eyes look distant for a minute as she ponders her options. I know she doesn't have other options. She doesn't comment, but slams the door behind her as she runs out into the cool night air.

I don't know where she's going but I can find out if necessary. After all, I put a tracker on her iPhone which I gave her a couple of years ago. So if she ever went somewhere questionable, I would know. I have access to her Apple account as well to help me keep tabs on her. You can never be too safe in today's world.

I am sure May's hesitation with Tianbao has to do with her playing with online dating. I noticed that she has been seeing a guy on the regular these past few months. I was thinking about commenting, but then I thought better of it. In her current mindset, expressing my disapproval would only drive her straight into the other man's arms. I'll let her have her fun for now. I'll find a way to take care of the guy when the time comes. She'll eventually realize that none of those losers online will match up to the man I have chosen for my good little May.

***

MAY LI

>Can you believe it?? My uncle tried to set me up again!

I texted furiously to Tanya. Twenty minutes later, a response.

>Who is it this time?

>Some tech guy from China (puke)

>Aren't you going to give the guy a chance?

>Not interested.

>Whatcha going to do then?

>Don't know, I tried to say no, but he's forcing me into it. And my other guy, I don't know what to do with him, he's not responding.

>Sorry to hear that. Find a way to get out of it then.

>Can't. Need to keep my job.

>Lol blackmail? Have to cook dinner for kids now, ttyl!

I can tell Tanya is weary of this conversation. Her answers are terse. She might have other priorities besides me right now, but that's okay. The conversation just gave me an idea. If my uncle is basically blackmailing me, what if I found some dirt to blackmail him?

***

WAITING FOR THE WORKDAY TO END FEELS LIKE TORTURE. I make compounds in the lab, weigh them out, analyze them, submit them and repeat. Just before heading out for the day, I go to the bathroom to take a leak. As I'm about to get up from the toilet seat, I recognize Tanya and Amber's footsteps echoing in the bathroom. They are having a quiet conversation. Out of curiosity, I stay in the stall and engage in some harmless eavesdropping.

"Did May tell you about her latest drama?" Tanya asks.

"About forced marriage? Yea, probably every colleague knows about it by now," Amber says sourly.

"It's ridiculous in this day and age. You know, sometimes I want to only half-believe her, it's like she is trying to get attention."

"Yea, well it does still happen in India. But May's family is something else. If you ask me, May and her uncle are both psycho," Amber jokes.

"Tell me about it! We're working for the top psycho in the world and friends with the psycho's pet." They both laugh. I can't believe they're actually making fun of me. Those bitches!

"I know, right? Like we have real problems, like children and mortgages. She's always complaining about her family drama as if her loaded uncle doesn't feed her enough. Meanwhile, we're working our asses off and have broken equipment that apparently her rich uncle can't afford to replace."

"Also, she has like 'compelled' family vacation to take care of all that crap. She always gets to skip work because of it. And this time, she was going on about how she would have to take a few weeks off for the engagement," Tanya shakes her head in disapproval.

"That's ridiculous. I would love some more vacation time!"

"And besides why do you let her treat you like that? She's always looking down on you. And then talking about her uncle's riches like they're candy."

"I don't know, she doesn't exactly listen to criticism. But she always expects us to be there for her."

"Exactly. She really is a piece of work. But I guess I feel sorry for her, she doesn't seem to have other friends."

They go into separate stalls and continue their conversations. I have heard enough of this betrayal. I stalk out of my stall and then out of the bathroom. These girls don't get it. After all the investment I put in those girls, telling them my personal problems, this is how they treat me. I was even going to put in a good word for them with my uncle. They should feel lucky to have me as a friend. They don't understand my suffering. They think they have problems; well, I'll give them problems when they are out on the streets begging for jobs.

***

I DIG AROUND ABOUT JINGLONG ON THE INTERNET but all the search results returned the same story of a self-made man who built a successful pharmaceutical company and is making important drugs to treat everything from cancer to liver diseases and inflammatory diseases. My phone vibrates twice, breaking my thoughts, but I pick it up.

"Hi mom, what is it?"

"Have you eaten dinner yet?" Her shrill voice pierces the quiet of my bedroom.

"Yeah mom, I did," I answer automatically, as I scroll through the latest feed on my social media pages, already bored of the same old conversations. A silence comes from the other end of the line.

"Jinglong told me that you met new man. How is he?" I want to hang up the phone right then and there, but I just grit my teeth and continue.

"He's fine mom, but I don't want to marry him."

"Aiya, why not?" Her high pitch comes through accusingly over the phone making me cringe.

"Ugh, he's not even Canadian! What, you expect me to move back to China with him?"

"Don't worry, Jinglong will get the paperwork through very fast, he'll be Canadian when he marries you."

"Mom, how many times do we have to go through this, I don't want to marry!"

"Xiao Mei, time is running out," she likes using my Chinese name when she is trying to convince me of something important. "I hear he is very good boy!"

"Mom, no! You can't make me! This is a life changing decision here."

"Aiya, stop being drama queen. Your uncle seems very serious about this boy, you should reconsider. Think of me, I want grandbabies."

"It's not always about you!"

"Is not about you either! You so selfish, think of all Uncle Jinglong done for you." I want to hang up again, but I thought of another idea.

"Okay, okay mom, by the way, do you know relatives from Jinglong's family well?"

"Huh? Why suddenly you ask?"

"You know, I'm just curious to hear some stories of how Jinglong became as successful as he is today."

"Ah good girl, who you want to talk to? Then you can be successful like him someday."

"Hmm, anyone you know really, relatives who were close with him in the past. I haven't really tried to connect with him before, but I want to try."

"Let me think. Yes, I have some contacts. Let me give them to you."

***

JINGLONG LI

Back at my condo, I check May's phone activity on my MacBook as a habit after dinner every day. She complains to her colleagues about me and her potential marriage partner, she complains about her work and she is getting her hair done this evening. Typical May activities so far.

I scroll through her calls and notice she made an unusually large number of calls today, particularly to China. What are you up to, May? Curious, I look up each of the numbers, and for the first time in a long time, fear creeps into my body. She called up my old acquaintances, and I'm sure it wasn't just social calls. She is barking up the same tree as my wife did back in the day. I will have to put an end to this nonsense.

As much as I don't like to admit it, I need May as much as she needs me. I don't want to lose her. She is my pillar in this world. After I lost my daughter, I was in a dark place for a long time, and I couldn't stay in China any longer without going insane. I kept replaying the last argument I had with my wife.

"You are insane! You know how it will affect our family if they knew? You will go to jail or worse! Think about our daughter, what will her future be like?"

"Su, everything I have done, I have done for this family."

"You say that Jinglong, but you did it because you are selfish! You just wanted the money. I can't believe I've been so blind!"

"You think I like selling opium in the streets? Money doesn't fall from trees! I work for ten, twelve hours a day, I work like a dog in the lab for what? You think I like it? I'm doing this for you and Mimi."

"No, I can't accept this. If you don't turn yourself in, I will walk away from you. You don't even spend time with us, what's the damn point?"

"Su, you will regret this! If it weren't for me, you wouldn't have a roof over your head, drugs for your pain and nice clothes to wear."

"Bullshit! You always think you're all that. You think you're in control of everything! But you're not, I'll live just fine without you!

"I'd like to see you last a day! You don't even work, you don't have any skills to work. The only thing you can do is be a housewife, and even then you're mediocre at best..."

The last argument haunts me still. I look over at the family picture on the bookshelf and reminisce about Mimi. I've done it all, begged, borrowed and stolen. Eventually, I made enough to have my own pharmaceutical company and move out here to Canada, looking for a fresh start. I would say I have redeemed myself for making useful, life-saving drugs now at fair market rates. Soon enough as my company grew, I could even afford to fly my family back and forth from China.

If only you realize, May, everything I have done, I have done for you. The full moon casts a luminous glow, reflecting off the bare hardwood floor and the black screen of the wide flat screen television. The condo feels empty without you, May. I gaze up at the moon wondering if you are admiring the same moon tonight.

***

MAY LI

Calling relatives and friends of Jinglong in China results only in dead ends. So I thought I would look closer to home. During lunch, I slip out and head to my uncle's apartment while he is out schmoozing with some American executives. I still have the keys to his condo since he never asked for them back. I sift through some documents in a filing cabinet and on his desk in his study. I also try looking for hidden compartments, but come up with nothing.

I glance at the photo of my late cousin Mimi and her mother framed on the bookshelf. I haven't thought about them for a while. I only have brief recollections of Mimi. We were close when we were young, but drifted apart as we grew up. I regret not seeing her before she passed. I can't imagine what she must have been going through when she decided to commit suicide. Her mother followed her out of grief. She was mentally unstable, as Jinglong had mentioned.

I realize suddenly that I had lost track of time and it has already been more than an hour since I arrived here. I hear the sound of a key being inserted into the front door. My heart starts pounding and I look around, desperate for somewhere to hide. I'm near the kitchen, so I slip into the walk-in pantry, hoping Jinglong wouldn't need anything from it. I hear his footsteps as he enters and wipes off his shoes. I peer through the small gap in the pantry door and watch Jinglong as he sits on the couch and switches on the TV. Just then, a knock comes at the door. A slight groan escapes Jinglong and he shuffles back towards the door.

"May I come in?" a high pitched woman's voice comes through the door.

"If you must."

I quietly shift inside the pantry so I can see the door. A woman dressed in a washed out hoodie and sweatpants steps through. Her hair is arranged in a low ponytail and her demeanor expresses exhaustion. It's the same look Tanya wears all the time.

"I need a higher monthly cheque. You don't return any of my calls."

"What is it this time, Amy?" He sounds weary.

"I have to support Stephanie you know, you are not paying enough child support. She's growing and..."

"I pay plenty. And as I said you cannot prove that she is my child. You just have to prioritize your expenses. I already increased your monthly rate by ten dollars last year." I can't believe what I am hearing. I pull out my phone and press record.

"Look, I came here because you promised us a better life. But all I see is empty promises. I don't have a job, I'm on food stamps and my daughter is struggling in school, but I can't help her. I would go back to China, but I don't have a home to go back to."

"I practically saved you from your shitty boyfriend back then. And I even flew you here to this country. What more do you want?"

"The boyfriend who you sold drugs to! You can't even give me paperwork to make me legal! You could at least show some support. Even a little shred of love to Stephanie. She doesn't have a father figure in her life."

"That doesn't sound like my problem."

"Oh yeah? You chose this when you decided to sleep with me while you were still married. I can tell people your secrets."

"So what? You knew I could never marry you, you chose to have the baby. You were just a random woman I met on the street. Part of the deal is that you disappear and tell no one about my past or our past. No one would believe you anyway."

"You will regret this." Her voice sounds strained, but she stands up straight.

"I hope you don't end up like my wife."

The woman walks out and slams the door behind her.

"And don't come back dirtying my apartment again!" I hear Jinglong add.

After a few minutes to collect himself, Jinglong enters the bathroom and shuts the door behind him. Soon after, I hear the shower faucet being turned on. I take this opportunity to escape the condo, locking the door quietly behind me. I run out as fast as I can, trying to catch the woman.

"Amy! Wait up! We should talk."

***

LATER THAT DAY, I PREPARE MYSELF TO HEAD to my uncle's apartment and confront him. I pace back and forth in my bedroom, the floor creaking with each step. My heart beats like a million drums and my palms are slick with cold sweat. I look at myself in the full length mirror, taking a few selfies to distract myself. I go through my walk-in closet, absentmindedly organizing my clothes. Maybe I shouldn't be doing this? After all, he has provided for me. What would my parents say when they find out the truth? No, I can't have doubts right now. I have to do it. It is for my freedom.

***

JINGLONG LI

After my morning jog and a cup of coffee, I settle down on a yoga mat for my daily meditation. I scarcely start my breathing exercises when there comes a hard knock on my door. I'm not expecting anyone, who could it

163

be? I hope it isn't Amy again. I let out a sigh and get up to receive my unwelcome guest. I look through the peephole and see May's face peering back. What a pleasant surprise, I didn't expect her to come so quickly. She must have come here to apologize for her earlier behavior.

She walks silently through the door, her body stiff. She looks simultaneously weary and defiant.

"I know about Amy," May says quietly.

I feel my pulse quicken but keep my cool as I always have in tough situations. It is as I have feared, but I quickly decide that it's best not to deny it.

"Oh? Did she fill your head with lies?"

"I don't think she's lying. In fact, I have proof."

"I don't know what you're talking about."

"Proof of your wife and daughter's death. You killed them. Why?" May accuses. I smile. May has always been inquisitive.

"You have to understand, they forced me. I had no choice. They were going to reveal everything about how I built my company."

"You built it on the backs of other people."

"And you happen to benefit from that." I'm losing her. I must explain to her why I did it.

"May, my dear. I loved them, my wife and daughter. I couldn't see them go down with me, it was better this way." It is true, I loved them. My wife was good to me, also obedient. Sometimes I would have to remind her of her place, but she always came around. I gave her some good old Miltown drug to control her hysteria. "But they forced my hand. We had a bad argument, and then my wife threatened to go to the police. I got desperate, I hit her on the head and she fell down the stairs. Mimi found out about her mother that day, as she overheard the argument. It was painful, but she resisted, so I made it look like suicide from grieving her mother's death. I do regret though, how much I miss them."

"It's too late now, I collected the evidence, and I will hand them over to the police. I have them ready to send. But if you give up trying to marry me off and help me find another job at a different company, I will destroy the evidence and never speak of this again." I laugh. Poor May, she thinks she can win the game by blackmailing me. But, I already saw this coming. I can't have May leave me. She's completely delusional!

"You're not afraid to end up like them?"

"If it means exposing you, no."

"I'm afraid I can't do that. You really are like a daughter to me. I've looked after you since you were sixteen. I just want to see you succeed in the best way possible."

"Then I guess I will have to turn you in." May's voice was wavering. Even if she had evidence, she would not have the guts to do it. But I won't leave it up to chance.

"I don't think that would be wise, May. You see, the rest of our relatives are dependent on my income. They reap from my benefits as much as you do. Do you really want to take that away from them?"

"They will be better off without you. You're just doing all this because you're selfish. You just want to control everyone, especially me!"

"May, you are getting this all wrong." I raise my voice, barely containing my anger. "It's for the good of everyone, especially you!"

"Me? Look at me, I'm not happy like this! I can't even be my own person or make any damn decisions in my life. You think I want this?"

I can see this argument going nowhere. A long silence stretches between us. I collect myself and speak in a calm voice, "It's not about what you want, May. Think of the rest of the family. My wife and daughter were sacrificed so I could build an empire. I have connections back in China who can easily remove your parents as well. An accidental slip in prescription pills is all it takes." I'm sorry it has come to this, May, but you leave me no choice. May falls silent.

"Why are you trying to ruin my life?" She struggles to steady her voice, but she trembles and looks down at her feet, tears welling up in her eyes. I really don't like making her cry, and I really do hate it when she does. I can't deal with a hysterical woman.

"Oh, my dear May, I don't want to ruin your life. I gave you everything. I was trying to protect you. I'm doing this out of love. You will understand eventually."

"Love? You call this love? You have no idea what love actually is. You won't get away with this!" May turns on her heel and the door slams behind her, leaving me once again alone in my empty apartment. I sigh, shaking my head, and I pick up the phone to dial a number.

At First Sight

By Margaret Woodford

"WHAT'S THAT RACKET? SOUNDS LIKE A DRUNKEN BRAWL." Ned hit the brakes, enveloping his black roadster in a cloud of red dust. "It's a little early for alcohol-infused fisticuffs, don't you think?"

Mac laughed, "It looks like a bit of a clash, alright. Maybe this is the local colour you promised."

Ned parked the car and jumped out. He leaned against the fender and gestured to Mac to join him. They peered through the raucous crowd.

"It looks like two guys pummeling each other," Mac remarked.

The sudden appearance of this stylish duo distracted the mob for just a moment. They returned their attention to the fray, egging on the combatants, "Come on, White. Hit him again!"

"That's it, Sid. Let her have it. Give it to her!"

Mac's eyes widened. "Give it to her? It sounds like one of those brawlers is a female!"

"Huh? What? Oh, that's probably the 'Big White One.' She has quite the reputation around here." Something caught Ned's attention and he blushed. "Never mind that now. Get a load of that doll in the red dress. No, don't gawk, just look to your left casual like."

Mac turned sideways and considered the young woman in red. She had dark shining hair and eyes and her smile displayed perfect teeth.

"Yeah, she's a looker alright, but tell me more about the Big White One. Why do they call her that?"

Ned shrugged and gazed at the dark eyed girl. She flashed a shy smile and returned her attention to the warriors, one of whom lay on the ground, while the other remained in battle stance. She rushed to the victor's side. "Hey, it looks like he's had enough. Are you okay, Livvie?"

"Is *she* okay?" the untidy pile at their feet croaked.

Liv addressed the pile, "Oh, you're alright, Sid. Allow me." She grasped his bleeding paws and pulled him to his feet. They stood nose to nose for several seconds. Liv smiled. "I hear you called me a hard case, so that's what you get, Sid." She shook soil from her torn denim overalls. "Isn't that right, May?"

The dark-haired girl sidestepped the dust storm. "You always hurt the ones you love."

"She must adore me, then!" Sid remarked. "But, Liv, I only agreed with Joe after you blackened his eye. He said you were case-hardened."

"Oh, like that makes a difference." Liv rolled her eyes. "Well, I expect my friends to defend my honour, so there's that. Anyway, no hard feelings." Sid flinched as she extended her hand. He gave it a feeble shake.

May tugged at Liv's sleeve. "Hey, Liv. Do you know those two fellas over there by the swanky motor?"

"Nope, but they look like a couple of dandies to me." She met Mac's amused gaze. "Nice smile," she muttered, "fancy duds."

"Let's introduce ourselves." Mac shoved Ned forward.

Sid caught Mac's remark as he was passing and warned, "You want to stay away from that Big White One. She's a harridan."

Liv rushed at him. "What did you say?"

Sid blanched. "Nothing, Liv. It's time I hurried on. I gotta be somewhere." He ran to catch up with his pals, muttering under his breath, "Someone needs to teach her a lesson."

Liv called after him, "Go get a wash. You stink like a buck goat!"

Mac approached the 'Big White One' and her friend, his hand outstretched in a gesture of peace. "Good afternoon, ladies?"

"Is that an observation or a question?" Liv ignored the hand. "I'm Olivia White. This is my friend, May Murphy."

May nodded. "You gentlemen new around here?"

"I'm from Lance Cove," Ned answered. "Mac just moved to Freshwater..."

Liv raised an eyebrow. "What is he, a fish?"

Mac laughed. "Freshwater Cove on the south side. Ned was just showing me around."

"Ooh. Fancy that! Welcome to the Front. We're pretty 'down to earth' around here!" Liv flicked red soil from her hair. "Come on May, let's go to Nick's. I'm starved."

"Ned tells me Nick's has great fish and chips. Mind if we tag along?" Mac asked.

With no reply, Liv and May headed toward the nearby 'restaurant,' a grey bungalow jammed between an outcrop of grey rock and a grey-pebbled beach. Nick's was a combination pub/pool hall/snack bar. The sign outside promised fresh fish and chips, cold beer, and live music. The live musicians were two retired fisher folk, one of whom keyed a piano accordion with gnarled fingers while the other bowed a fine old violin. These two gents could play anything, as long as it was a waltz.

Mac and Ned followed the girls. "How's the beer?"

"I wouldn't know," Liv replied. "We never drink the stuff." She and May took a seat at a table for two and Liv swung her feet onto the neighbouring table, blocking it off. "Hey, Rocky! Two fish and chips and a couple Cokes over here."

Mac and Ned selected stools at the counter. "Do you get the feeling we're not welcome?" Ned remained silent, so Mac waved to get his attention and asked, "Hey, what's your problem, Bubbles? You've gone all taciturn and mysterious." Mac winked. "Must be love. Can't be the weather." Catching the barman's eye, he called out, "Two beers over here, Sir. Thanks."

Ned turned his seat on an angle and stole covert glance at May. Liv called out, "Ain't she a looker, fellas? She could be a movie star, what?" May's cheeks burned and she glared at her friend.

Mac caught Liv's eye and winked, "A real beauty, alright!"

She whispered to May, "Oh no, not another one."

"Ignore them, Liv. Maybe they'll go away."

"Good idea." She followed her friend's advice and finished her fish and chips.

"How about you drive me home? I need to clean up. I smell like a bad tooth." Liv waved as she and May headed for the door. "See ya, Rocky."

"What are you doing tomorrow?" Ned called.

Liv tossed him a reply, "We'll be at Seaside Park in the afternoon."

May nudged her and whispered, "Why did you tell them that?"

"I don't know. They might be…interesting."

They stepped outside, leaving Mac and Ned sitting at the counter. After a few seconds, when Ned went to follow, Mac grabbed his arm. "How about a game of pool or another beer, buddy? Or, you can trot along after them if you want but that's not *my* style."

"Sure, Mac, and I suppose the dolls frisk around you like puppies," Ned muttered, then plopped onto the stool. "Alright, you go rack 'em up."

"Now, now, bud. No need to get bitter. I just haven't found a puppy I want to bring home to Mother, but that 'Big White One,' she's more like a wolf cub. I wonder how dear old Susan would react if I brought Liv home to dinner."

"From what I've seen of your mother, I wouldn't tempt fate. She might slip your new girlfriend a mickey or throw her an old bone. Anyway, isn't your ma more of a cat person?" Then he added, "Jeez, old man. Don't tell me you're smitten with that Liv character. She seems as wild as a loon and did you notice her socks? They're odder than she is. I'm sure she was wearing her father's old work boots. Now, May on the other hand, I can't picture her streeling around covered in dust or scraping her manicure on some guy's teeth. She seems too ladylike and sensible for that."

"Pity," said Mac as he watched Liv climb into May's battered red coupe.

***

MAY GUNNED THE ENGINE, SPRAYING DUST AND GRAVEL.

"Now, take it easy driving," Liv warned.

"You don't want to be late for supper, do you?"

"I don't want to be dead for supper either. Then I'd really be late and Mom would kill me! Anyway, I'm as full as an egg after that feed."

They sped along the hilly coastal road, bouncing around the twists and turns. "What do you make of Mac and Ned? They're not like our usual crowd," May remarked.

"I don't know. They sure do dress snappy. Mac is prettier than I am, and you could slice cheese with his trouser crease."

May lifted an eyebrow. "Interesting. I never heard such glowing praise from you before."

"I still say they look like a couple of dandies, though," Liv laughed.

They stopped in front of a weathered yellow saltbox overlooking the sea. Liv jumped from the car and May sped away in her usual spray of gravel and dust.

On Sunday afternoon, May and Liv sat with their girlfriends at the park by the sea. A group of children sploshed about in a small brook that gurgled across the beach. Blue jays scolded from the trees and wild ponies grazed outside the fence.

A booming voice broke the serenity, "Well, well, well, Ned. Here's May. And who have we here?" Mac and Ned stood awaiting an introduction.

"And three wells make a river!" Liv got to her feet, which were clad not in work boots, but in pretty, low-heeled shoes.

Mac's smile froze as he studied this well-dressed girl. That couldn't be the 'Big White One,' could it? The sun highlighted her golden-brown hair and brought out the green in her eyes. For just a split second, Mac was speechless.

"What? Oh, hiya, Liv. I didn't recognize you. You changed your hair.

Weren't you a redhead yesterday? Ned, didn't you think she was a redhead?" Mac asked.

"I thought she was a redhead. She's not a redhead."

"My hair was red from the dust yesterday. This is me after my weekly wash."

Mac smiled at Liv, "Anyway, you clean up well."

"Thanks. You're not so bad, yourself."

Ned settled on the bench between May and one of her friends, while Mac and Liv found a spot beneath a flowering linden tree.

"So, Liv, how do you spend your time when you're not thrashing your boyfriends?" Mac joked.

"Well, I help with my younger siblings. There are ten kids in my family and four of them are younger than me, so you know, general sibling entertainment, and I love to read, especially folklore and mythology."

"Well, an intellectual. I'm impressed."

"So, what about you?" Liv asked. "What are you into besides tormenting the innocents?"

"I'm an electrician by trade, but photography is my great love. I develop my own photos."

May stood up and called, "Hey, Liv, we're hungry. What time's lunch?"

Liv frowned, "Interruptions, interruptions! Well, I guess we should feed the youngsters. There's plenty of grub if you and Ned want to join us. I brought forty-mile-an-hour buns."

"Why do you call them that? What kind of buns are they?" he asked.

"They're my mother's tea biscuits. We call them that because they go so fast," she laughed.

May and Liv spread a large blanket on the grass and unloaded the picnic lunch. Ned planted himself next to May and the sandwich tray. Mac and Liv sat with their heads together and when they had finished their lunch, Mac got to his feet. "I think I'll take a stroll to the lighthouse. Ned tells me it's a beautiful spot."

"It is, but you should never go walking alone around here," Liv warned. "There are fairies and ghosts. Why do you think I wear odd socks?"

"Okay, then, you can fill me in on the local folklore. I have my camera, so I might take a few snaps. Come on." He slung a leather bag over his shoulder and offered his hand.

They headed out of the park and followed a narrow road leading to the woods.

"Where do you think they're going, Ned?" May stood up. Her brow furrowed. "I've never seen Liv go off with a fella by herself before. I mean, she doesn't even know him. Mac is trustworthy, right?"

Ned shrugged. "I suppose so. I only met him a couple of weeks ago, but he seems all right. A bit sure of himself, but Liv can take care of herself, can't she."

May sat down. "I guess you're right."

***

"SO, WHAT'S WITH THE ODD SOCKS, THEN, LIV?" Mac asked as they made their way through the clover-scented meadow. The wild ponies scattered at their approach.

"I don't want the fairies to lead me astray. They're all around here you know. We call them 'the little people.' They lead you into the woods or the marsh, and then when the fog rolls in, you lose your way. Some people disappear entirely, and others turn up days later unable to remember what happened. But," she waggled a warning finger under his nose, "if you wear odd socks or turn your clothes inside out, they won't take you away."

Mac glanced at Liv's shoes. "You're not wearing odd socks today. Aren't you afraid they'll get you? How do you know I'm not a little fella sent to lure you into the woods?"

Liv dipped her hand into the pocket of her dainty jacket. "Ha! Mr. Fairy, you won't get me. I brought a magic bun. Besides, you're too tall." She dropped the soggy lump into her pocket.

"Okay, I dare you to follow that trail and we'll see," he indicated a barely discernible rut at the edge of the meadow.

"I've never noticed this path before. Maybe it's a rabbit trail." Liv took Mac's hand and led him into the cool, piney woods. "Not all fairies are bad you know. Some just like to play tricks, like the pixies who steal money and children's toys. One day, Mom's new sweater disappeared from her bedroom. She swears some little person went off with it. Then there are the brownies, who like to help folks, but you have to leave little gifts for them, or they can turn on you."

"Do you really believe this stuff?" Mac grinned.

"You better not be laughing at me. Maybe I'll have to teach you a lesson."

"Or, maybe not," he replied. His expression darkened.

"Maybe not," she answered. "You never know, I might be leading you astray."

"Yeah, you're a pixie and this is your enchanted path. I'm pretty sure I've been fairy struck." Liv blushed as his smile returned and crinkles gathered around his eyes.

"Anyway, there's the lighthouse." She led the way towards the weather-beaten sentry on the headland and they settled on the cool grass.

The North Atlantic boomed on the rocks beneath the cliff and a fog bank loomed on the horizon. The lighthouse beacon flashed, daring the mist to draw closer. A lone gannet called a warning as it dipped in and out of the grey.

Mac pulled a box camera from his knapsack and took photos of the lighthouse and the coastline. He even had the audacity to sneak a few profile shots of Liv as she gazed out to sea.

She looked out of the corner of her eye at Mac's camera aimed in her direction and suppressed a smile. "How do you think a black eye would suit you?" She turned to face him. "Some photographer you are. You have your thumb over the lens! Anyway, why can't you just enjoy the scenery?"

"Oh, but I *am* enjoying the scenery. I really am!"

Liv stood up. "That fog bank is moving in. We should head back before the horn blows. It'll blast our ear drums if we're too close."

They took a different path on the way back and as they strolled through an open field, Mac pointed to a lone pine tree. "Hey, Liv, do me a favour and go stand over there. It'll make a great shot."

Liv obliged and stood fidgeting beneath the tree as Mac rummaged through his knapsack. "Hurry up before I take root, and keep your thumb away from that lens," she scolded.

"Okay. Ready." Mac turned toward her, his face serious.

Liv blanched and cold water traveled along her spine. "But, that's... that's not your camera!"

Mac pointed a silver revolver directly at Liv's face, "I'm going to shoot you, now." His eyes were cold and the crinkly laugh lines had disappeared.

"No! Please, no!" Liv fell to her knees, "Please don't!"

He squinted his eyes and aimed the weapon, his face deadly serious, as

Liv cried and begged for her life.

"I got a bead on ya. Say your prayers!"

Liv stared into his eyes, her face streaked with tears. "That's not funny! Why are you doing this?"

Mac lowered the gun and pulled the trigger. Nothing happened. "It's not real," he laughed. "You should see the look on your face!"

Liv scrambled to her feet. "You sick bastard! I'll kill you!"

Mac shrugged and walked away. "I just thought someone should teach you a lesson."

Brown-Skinned Man

By Evena Hewitt

MY MOTHER'S FLIGHT FROM HER HOME WAS UNEXPECTED.

It was a late evening in 1965, just before sunset. Earlier, my mother and I had spent time together. I watered her flower gardens while she straggled along.

"Would you like to help mum?"

"Oh no thank you, Rose."

"Feeling any better, mum?"

"Oh yes."

Without notice, she strolled to the rear of the house. In a few minutes she returned with a few freshly picked guavas. She bit into one.

"Delicious," she said.

"That one is for you." She stretched out her hand.

We stood there munching on the ripe guavas when a cricket's chirps broke the spell. I held her hand.

"Mum," I said. "Time to go in. I have an homework assignment." She nodded.

We walked up the steps.

"Wait," she said. "Roses for the center or coffee table."

I fetched the clippers from behind the pot of crotons on the step. I clipped several roses. I raised the bunch of pink roses for her approval.

"Okay, mum?"

"Some fern," she added.

"Go inside, mum. This won't take long."

Eventually, I returned to the house, filled the vase with water. I set the vase in the center of the table on the white crocheted doily. She crinkled her eyes.

"No water dripped on the mahogany table, mum."

I started my literature assignment about the social climber Rebecca Sharp in Vanity Fair and her difficulty of breaking into high society because of her low birth. And I thought about my father and his brown-skin, my mother and her black skin. Once, I overheard my mother complaining to her sister Vi.

"Nothing I could do right for that man," she said. "He just wanted my father's money. I am not brown enough."

My mother became restless, walking to and fro.

"Time for your soap opera, mum," I said.

She sauntered over to the radio to listen to her favourite radio soap opera. She fiddled with the knobs before raising the volume. Afterwards, she drew the rocking chair closer to the radio. I could tell the soap had finished when she came over to my chair. She lingered over my shoulder.

"Ready for bed?" I asked.

"Not yet." She tapped my head. She returned to the living room.

I glanced up from my homework. She stood at an open window, looking up into the dark sky. I heard her humming her favourite hymn, "All Things Bright and Beautiful."

On completion of my homework, I dug out *Lady Chatterley's Lover*, covered in brown wrapping paper from behind the china cabinet. Don't let that evil book cross his doorstep, my father said.

"Sinful," he said.

With a two week's loan from the adult section in the library, and my father's warning, I felt compelled to read as quickly as possible. And after my nightly read, I prayed to God to absolve my sins.

That night, distracted by its content, I forgot about keeping an eye on my mother.

A click of the living room door lock broke my concentration. Thinking it was my father returning home, I pushed my chair back, threw the book behind the cabinet. When I did look up, the door was wide open. My mother gone.

"Mum, mum. Where are you?"

In the darkness, all I could hear were her footsteps retreating in the distance.

"Mum, it's me, Rose. Wait a minute."

As if in a dream, my mother offered no sign of recognition. She ran up a dirt track with cane fields on either side.

In desperation, I ordered her to stop. She ignored me.

She hitched up her dress, disappeared into a field of canes. I listened as she brushed aside the cane stalks. Then silence fell.

I thought I still heard movement among the canes. But it was only a nightly breeze fanning the cane leaves. I might have stayed a few moments longer. But my fear of duppees or ghosts, heart men and hags, I fled home.

"Nita, Nita, mum's gone," I cried.

Nita, the housekeeper with her plump round face scanned me up and down.

"What do you mean gone? I just lef the two of you out dey," she said as she slipped into the island dialect which my father banned from our home. "Looka my crosses tonight." Nita conducted a search of the house. "Dear Jesus, help me."

"I told you. She's not in this house. She ran away."

I made some rude remark about not understanding. Nita flinched, raised her eyebrows.

"What happen?" she pointed at me.

"I forgot to remove the key from the front door."

"How many times ya father and me tell ya to hide dat key?"

"I know. She seemed ok to me. Here's the key."

She placed it in her skirt pocket. "This is nothing but trouble."

"We've got to call the police," I said.

"Na, na, na", she said, "I'll get into big trouble with Mr. C. He wouldn't be able to hold up in his head in public. And your poor mother would be called a madwoman for the rest of her life."

"I don't care about the public or his friends. I care about my mother."

I grabbed the telephone to contact the police. Nita removed it from my hand, dropped it on its rest.

"Now listen to me, I want you to calm ya self down, I older than you and know more about these tings. When ya father come home I'll tell him. OK? Now go lie down."

I went to my room, flopped into bed and wept. A few minutes later, Nita poked her face around my door.

"Come, I mek some hot cocoa for you. Want some pound cake with it? I mek some today."

***

IN THE DINING ROOM, WE SAT NEXT TO EACH OTHER.

"She was so good to me. She was so good to my whole family. I could be in England all like now so, working as a nurse. That's why my mother sent me here in 1956. But I met a wretched man named Earl, got me pregnant, married me. And ya know what he disappeared to America. Never heard a word from that man. I shouldn't be telling you dese tings, though. Ya mother tek me back. And I've been with her ever since. I luv ya mudda, so much."

She drew me close to her. I fell into her arms. I sobbed. I held on to her tighter than ever.

"Thank you for telling me about mum."

From the age of eight, Nita became my surrogate mother. My mother spent her day managing her different businesses.

"We'll find her." She rubbed my back.

As she held me, I looked up at the glass framed Jesus on the dining room wall. I forgot how much I disliked him holding forth in our house. I prayed for my mother.

***

That night, tired as I was, I willed myself to stay awake. When the clock chimed 11pm and the radio played God Saved Our Gracious Queen, I realized my father wouldn't be home any time soon. I got up, switched off my bedroom light, went to sleep.

I spent a restless night, tossing and turning. I dreamt of huge waves sucking me out to sea with me scrambling to the surface for air. Suddenly I sat up in bed when a rooster crowed to announce early dawn.

I stayed awake for a while. I opened the wooden jalousies on either side of the glass windows to let in the early morning air. I peeped out. But the coconut and golden apple trees blocked my view to the road. Disappointed, I returned to bed and fell into a deep sleep.

***

MORNING ARRIVED WITH SUNLIGHT BRIGHTENING MY ROOM. In the kitchen, Nita banged pots and pans. And on cue, I heard her grumble as she marched to my room.

"Rose, get up."

"Is my dad home yet?"

"Yes, he is practically all dressed. Just needs to put his tie on. He is on the verandah reading the morning newspaper."

"And he knows about mum, right?"

"Yes. I heard him talking quietly on the phone. Now don't ask me any more questions. Just get ready for school."

***

IN ABOUT HALF OF AN HOUR, I appeared at the table dressed in my school uniform, yellow skirt, white blouse with tie, black oxfords, white socks. My hair combed in a braided ponytail.

"Good morning, dad."

"What a glum face, girl. Cheer up, you could do better than that. She'll come home. Where can she hide on such a small island?" He adjusted his tie. "We'll soon find her."

He bowed his head, said grace, poured tea from the china teapot, cracked his egg, buttered his bread. We ate in silence. Pushing his chair back, he said he expected to see me seated in the car.

"In ten minutes."

"Yes, dad."

I swallowed hard to keep myself from crying. This was not the father I had grown to love, the one who on a cloudless night pointed out the Big and Little dipper, the Milky way to me.

***

THE MINI MORRIS SITTING IN THE DRIVEWAY was for all intents and purposes mine while my father searched for a new one. Before entering the car, I walked to the end of the driveway to check the street. Only a bunch of giggling elementary school children walked past. They wished me a good morning.

"Getting late. Time to go. Come, get in the car."

***

ON OUR RIDE TO MY GIRLS' SCHOOL IN THE CITY, my father babbled on. I detected a whiff of alcohol despite the mint he chewed. I screwed up my face.

"What you doing that for?" he said.

"Nothing," I replied. "Dad, please, can we talk about mum?"

"Stop biting your finger nails. So unladylike!" I shrank at his rebuke. Then, held my hands in my lap. "I know what you're going to ask me. I've got a few people keeping an eye out for her."

"An eye? How about the police?" He slammed on the brake, signaled, parked.

Gesticulating with his index finger, he warned me never to contact the police.

"If this is exposed, I wouldn't be able to hold up my head on this island." My stomach grumbled. It heaved. I released the door handle, ran to the side of the road-emptied my breakfast in a patch of khus khus grass. He remained seated in the car.

"You better now?" He asked as he passed me his white monogrammed handkerchief.

"Yes," I lied. I really wanted to say I had lost trust in him, respect for him. I bit my lips. I felt the warm blood in my mouth.

"Wipe your face. By the way, I have a late evening appointment so Evelyn's mother will drive you home. You are so soft. You take everything to heart. Boys are stronger. I wish your mother gave me a boy." Those words stung.

***

UPON ARRIVAL AT THE SCHOOL GATE, I gathered up my school bag and gym clothes from the back seat. Then, I stuck my head through his window.

"Did you ever really love my mother? Or did you love her money more? And have you ever loved me since I'm not the boy you hoped for?"

He winced.

"And another question dad, why didn't you seek professional help for my mum, your wife, dad?"

He raised two fingers to his lips.

"Don't tell me to hush."

"Rose," he whispered. "Lower your voice. We don't want the world to know, do we?"

"Who is we, dad? You can't keep pulling the wool over my eyes. I'm seventeen years old. It's always about your pride."

"I'll search for her. You go along," he said. He shifted into first gear. He drove off.

Without a backwards glance, I moved on.

***

MY MOTHER, A TALL, WELL-OFF CHEERY BLACK WOMAN married my father, an educated brown-skinned man whose family had nothing, as my aunt Vi mockingly repeated.

"They didn't even had two pennies to rub together. She married the wrong man." Throughout my life, whenever tension arose between my parents, those words returned to haunt me. Was it his brown skin, I asked myself?

***

IT WAS DIFFICULT TO CONCENTRATE after that suspicious conversation with my father. And throughout morning classes, my stomach rebelled. At lunchtime, I hurried from my class to a secluded spot with my best friend Evelyn.

"What's the matter with you?" she asked.

"Nothing." The stored tears rushed down my cheeks.

"It's my mum. Last night she ran away from home. We don't know where she is. Suppose she's dead."

"Huh."

"She was sick." I went on to relate the whole story about my mother's breakdown, my father's refusal to seek help.

"I hate that man," I said.

"You don't think you're carrying it too far?"

"No. He's a selfish, prideful man."

"We'll look for her."

She opened her lunch box, offered me a sandwich. And true to her word, at the end of the school day, Evelyn and I walked up and down the main city streets searching. It was all for nothing.

***

DAYS RAN INTO WHAT SEEMED LIKE WEEKS. One evening, my father sat on the verandah in the rocking chair, with the ubiquitous drink in hand. I went out, stood in front of him.

"Excuse me dad, don't you think it's time you notified the police and my aunt Vi, my mother's sister?"

"What? You joking, right?"

"No."

He pitched the glass at the wall. I ducked. It shattered into tiny pieces with its contents spilling at my feet.

"Get out of here," he howled. "When is the last time I spanked you?" He removed his belt from his waist. I stared him in the face. His eyes were blood shot.

I said slowly and quietly, "If you so much as touch me, I will call the police." He stepped back.

"You're just like your mother."

Nita came running out to the verandah. "What's going on out here? You alright, Rose. Now go in your bedroom."

She fetched the broom. From my room, I could hear Nita sweeping and singing her favourite Pentecostal hymn, "All for Jesus, I Surrender."

A car door slammed shut. My father did not return to the next morning.

***

THE FOLLOWING WEEK, MY FATHER CONFRONTED me about leaking the family business. He bemoaned the fact people were talking behind his back.

"And you know what. A friend of mine had the nerve to say I drove my wife crazy. A big lie that is! You and your mother have brought shame to the family."

"Do you truly believe that, dad? When you married her, she didn't bring shame. She brought money. And you know it."

"I should have married somebody brown skinned like me."

"And poor." For that, I continued, "I will contact the police." He could only grind his teeth.

He blocked my way. He stunk of soured rum. One touch from my finger could have sent him sprawling to the ground. Instead, I bent my shoulders to pass under his arms.

***

AFTER CONTACTING THE POLICE, I instructed Nita to send for my mother's sister Vi, a widowed, devout, church organist who lived in a small village in the country. By the time the police arrived, I could hear the loud snores coming from my father's room. In the midst of giving a statement to the police, my chest tightened. I collapsed.

***

WHEN I AWOKE, AUNT VI AND NITA WERE STANDING on either side of my bed.

"Thank you, Jesus, ya back," Nita said. They looked worried.

The room reeked of disinfectant. I noticed two oxygen tanks, IV stand with me hooked up to them. Occasionally, a woman in cap and apron darted in and out of the room.

"Where am I?"

"You are in the hospital. We thought you were going to die." Aunt Vi wiped her tears.

"And mum?" Nita and my aunt turned towards each other. Dumbstruck.

"She died. Didn't she? I had a dream where I saw her wading into the sea at Sunset Beach. I stood on the shore. She turned and waved. She kept wading into the turquoise waters. As she moved farther and farther away, the colour of the water became darker and darker. Then there was a sudden flash, you know, just like when the sun vanishes at sunset?"

She vanished.

"That was only a dream," they intoned.

"That was only a dream."

Was it?

The Insatiable Lust of Madmen

By Sterling Mahl

"I'LL TELL YOU EVERYTHING YOU WANT TO KNOW, JUST DON'T HURT me, please…" I whimpered to the hideous brute holding a scalding red pair of iron tongs inches from my nose. The flickering shadows cast upon his face by a pair of tall candles left standing precariously on a nearby table created the frightful impression he didn't have a mouth – which was nonsense, since he'd just threatened to pull out my tongue. Time stood still as he likely pondered what to think of me. I just hoped that, beneath the crude exterior display of his modest station, he was the kind of man who appreciated cooperative subjects and would reciprocate in kind.

"Good lad," he cooed, patting my cheek none too gently and pulling back the tongs close to his own face as if comforted by the heat that emanated from them. He took a step back and revealed a wide smile full of rotting teeth that more or less matched the salt and pepper shade of his unkempt moustache. "You'n me gots lotta talk about, so let's get a head start, awright?"

Yes, all right, though frankly this was all going a little fast for my personal taste. Little more than an hour ago I'd been getting the day started with a mindless task – grinding locusts into aphrodisiac jelly to spice up late summer feasts up in the Palace – and here I found myself now shackled at all extremities and singing for my life in the basement of a rustic bawdy house. Or maybe this was the old harbour barracks the Navy abandoned after it stopped training sailors in favour of dragon riders, but I could swear a hint of spiced body lotion and wet cunt was seeping through from the floors above. Now don't get me wrong, I don't mean to pass judgement upon any man's taste in filthy pleasures; it just seemed fitting for scum revolutionaries to find shelter in the bowels of a whorehouse.

"Awright?" he insisted.

I vigorously nodded in agreement.

"Good. Now, this fella over there…" he hooked his thumb back towards a dark silhouette sitting a few meters behind him outside the reach of the candlelight and who, I believe, was the man who had brought me here against my will. "This fella he tells me you're an associate of the Master Callaghan, is that right? You're his apprentice, is that right?"

Right it was. I nodded again.

"Word 'round from the Palace is of a nasty weapon coming up in the works, is that right?"

Right again, but the truth is there was always something nasty being cooked up in Master Callaghan's laboratory. I'd seen enough experimental burning ointments and mind-altering concoctions for the past wars and the next. Odds were fair their information was pointing to the same project I was thinking of, though if this portly henchman's interrogation skills proved a faithful reflection of the Unsung Rebellion's infiltration network, I could probably afford to breathe a little easier and so decided to try my luck at being the cleverest man in the room.

"*The weapon?* Is that what you people are calling it?"

He looked confused. "Yes... does it have another name?"

The project did have a name – Scorched Vine – which was irrelevant for the time being.

"No, that's just the thing... we don't really talk about it as if it were an object."

"What is it, then? What's it do?"

"Well... it's not really something one would think of as –"

He rushed the tongs back to my face and snapped the tips three times in quick succession. "What's it do, boy!"

"Nothing. It does nothing."

"You working on a weapon that's do nothing?" He exhaled a short laugh. "Do I look like a fool to you?"

I decided not to answer that. "I'm telling you, it does nothing. It doesn't even exist! Master Callaghan's been talking about it like he's tweaking the last rivet on his prototype, but that's just to placate the Queen. All he's got is a plan, an idea... to kill everyone in Dravengoth. But he doesn't know how to do it. I swear!"

He stared at me with wary eyes, ostensibly weighing my version of events against what he'd expected to hear, possibly considering whether sticking rods of burning iron up my nostrils would help corroborate what he thought he knew of the Queen's madness.

"No weapon?" he asked, possibly rhetorically.

"That's what I said," I answered, nevertheless. "He's desperate to come up with a doomsday device that will finish off the war before the scouts even make it out of the stables, but right now, it's nothing but a concept."

"Then what's it do? You stop playing tricks on me!"

"He wants to create tiny particles that infiltrate people's bodies to make them sick –"

"Like a poison?"

"Yes, like a poison. You get the idea, but that's also all he's got: an idea. You see, most poisons have antidotes, or they won't affect everyone the same way, or they could lose some of their potency if you have to produce it on the scale necessary to annihilate an entire kingdom..." He looked as if I was speaking a foreign tongue. "You'd need to gather tons of rare ingredients and hundreds of people mixing them for several weeks to make enough poison. If any of them screwed up a batch or two, the *weapon* could lose half of its intended punch. Of course, that would still be better than nothing… but that's not what the Queen wants."

"So what kind of poison is it, then?"

That's where I came in, though I didn't see the need to reveal my personal involvement.

"I know we keep using that word but it's not a poison." His wide-open eyes shot lightning and he snapped the tongs. "Sorry… I… he wants to create a living poison."

The words appear to hang in the air, dancing in front of the man's eyes, intelligible but inaccessible.

"Thess no such thing."

Actually, there was. Unbeknownst to even the master, I was close to making it a reality. So unbearably close in fact, I'd bent my scientific curiosity sideways in favour of stalling the final stage of research once it became obvious what was growing in those petri dishes, and the only purpose it could be used for.

"You're right, there's no such thing." Yet. "Only in Master Callaghan's dreams."

"Will he be able to make it work?"

Although the only instinct that guided my answer at the time was self-preservation, in retrospect this turned out to be one of those life-defining moments, when one has to take in the whole landscape in a single glance and decide which side of the fence to stand on.

"Yes, I believe he can."

The man spun to look at his companion sitting in the shadow, leaving me to ponder whether telling the truth – or at least as close to it as I would dare – had unsealed the death sentence I had earned earlier this morning. It was still quite early in the day; the master wouldn't miss me for several hours if he kept to his daily rituals. Odds were, though, he'd come seeking answers once he found out the man he'd sent me out to kill was still roaming the halls. The short explanation is, I'm an alchemist, not an assassin, and sneaking into the Palace's kitchens to sprinkle the sole order of Eggs Benedict with a pinch of Nakrofix proved to be a task beyond my recognised skills. A kitchen boy viciously kicked my knee before I could even try to explain why I was hovering over the stove. I went down looking for an open fire, or perhaps a running basin to get rid of the vial in my hand but the boy and a passing cleaning wench then started hitting me with pots and pans until the cook connected all the dots – a cleverer fellow than most courtiers gave him credit for, he was – and fetched my victim, the man currently in the shadow. Likely he's an important figure, for he had no qualm drawing his dagger in plain view of the assembled bystanders, and he was about to slit my throat when I revealed sheepishly this ill-fated plot was of my master's bidding. He asked if I meant the Master Callaghan. I nodded, my face caked in snot and dried blood. He dragged me up to my knees and instructed the kitchen staff to forget the incident; he'd be dealing most severely with my insolence in private. He brought me down to the cold stores, stuffed me like a ragdoll in an empty wine barrel and told me to be quiet. Half an hour later here I was, playing mind games in a damp basement with a clumsy thug intent on bringing down the royal House of Barrettmoore.

The hushed conversation between my captors seemed to have reached a dead end. I heard the brute whisper something about sending me back. Did he mean the Palace? I could play that game as well as anyone: *Yes, I swear your secret is safe. I didn't even get a good look at any of you.* But the man in the shadow was having none of it.

'*He's seen my face, that's too great of a risk,*' I thought I heard him say.

They argued a few seconds longer before he came towards me and revealed he was indeed my assassination target. He was a tall, muscular specimen with the cheekbones of a princeling and all the good looks that open doors otherwise shut to the rest of us schlubs. I knew his type. In more casual circumstances he would have walked to me with a grin on his face, cut off a lock of my hair with his dagger and thanked me for my service before slicing my throat in one swift gesture. But these circumstances were far from casual, and he looked unpleasantly resigned.

"Do you know who I am?" he asked.

"No," I replied without hesitation. "The master only said to poison the eggs."

"Good. We'll be going back to the Palace, you and I. You will speak of what happened here to no one. You will tell your master you acted as he bid you, no more no less. You will see me coming and going, and if anyone asks you who I am, you will say that you don't know. Do you understand me?"

"Yes."

"Good." He spun deftly and disappeared in silence up the stairs.

***

NO, THIS CLEARLY WOULDN'T DO. What I needed was a magic bottomless bag. Expecting anyone to leave behind even half of Goldorf's nineteen-volume *Compendium of Applied Transmogrification* was beyond the reasonable limits of cruelty, but the realisation I may be able to carry only two, three at most, of the thick leather bound tomes before the pouch on my back started pulling me backwards left me to reconsider my plan. Did I really need to bolt before sundown? Maybe I could arrange for the other sixteen volumes to follow me later. No, that would leave a trail. I needed to focus and sort out the essential items. Common equipment – vials, beakers, cloth filters – was easy to replace with help from the right sponsor. It was the rare ingredients I kept neatly sealed in crystal jars that would take years to replenish. Maybe I could risk storing the dry components in small cotton pouches: easy to carry and better than nothing. How long does mandrake –

A rap at the door froze me in place.

Damn! They'd said someone would be in touch with further instructions but... this quickly? I'd been back in my chambers for barely twenty minutes after they'd carried me back up the hill, again uncomfortably packed up in the empty wine cask.

"Just a minute!" I yelled towards the door while I shoved the travel bag under the bed. Satisfied nothing left in sight would signal my intention to flee, I opened the door half-heartedly and started breathing again upon laying eyes on my master's servant.

I'd expected he might call upon me himself given the sensitivity of the murderous task he'd assigned mere hours earlier, but it was Aida, as usual, who delivered the summons to his laboratory. Sweet relief, I needed a short lustful interlude to get my mind back on track. I knew she'd be anxious to get back right away – the master was not a very patient man – but nevertheless extended a hand suggestively inviting her inside.

"How much time do we have?" I asked.

"Not now, Christopher."

She'd started using my given name – only in private, of course – after the second time we'd laid together. Maybe the first encounter wasn't enough to convince her there would be more, I didn't question it. But it had been five days since our last tryst and I could hardly think of anything else whenever she was nearby.

"I can't focus... The wait is driving me crazy."

She glanced quickly at the empty hall behind her and came close enough for me to smell the vinegar-based cleaning solution off her clothes. I started breathing heavily with unbridled anticipation.

"Have you been pleasuring yourself?" I shook my head rapidly back and forth while mouthing a silent 'no'. She'd forbidden it. "Have you touched another with those filthy hands of yours?" Well, technically I had. The master's work routinely required experimentation on live subjects, and the city guard kept us well-stocked by rounding up begging orphans – boys and girls – whenever the square got overcrowded. But that didn't count, so I shook my head again. She bit her lower lip and reached down my britches. I yelped.

"That's it, keep it right there and maybe you can have me tonight," she said, grabbing my cock with a firm grip. "Now screw your head back on because the master wants to see you immediately. His mood is fouler than I've seen it in weeks."

***

I MOVED FAST AFTER SHE LEFT, though it would be more accurate to say I was thrown into chaos. The master's mood likely had to do with my botched assassination attempt. Did that mean his position and status at court were now in question? Although the man in the shadow knew who was behind the poisoned eggs, the master was still blind to this morning's machination, including my coerced indoctrination into the Unsung Rebellion's network of informants. He wouldn't be for long, but hopefully I'd need him to remain in the dark only for the next twelve hours. By this time tomorrow, a merchant ship would reach the halfway marker between the isle of Capnor and the continent while he finished his usual late breakfast and instructed Aida to – oh shit! Aida. Should I ask her to come with me? What if she... No. I had no time to waste on *what if* scenarios right now. I'd just have to explain the whole imbroglio tonight and put forward my most convincing arguments.

The door to the master's laboratory was ajar. I could hear him speak – to himself most likely – in hushed tones. He sounded like he was... like he was commenting on a text laid out in front of him. "And how do you figure we'll be able to... ah, yes I see. Very clever you are, old boy... No, that won't work but we can get around it..."

I cleared my throat.

"Gaultier! Here you are, get in. Close that door." I complied. He looked frazzled, to be sure, but Aida had overstated his disposition. "I was just looking over your notes. You're further along than I thought. We may yet come out in one piece."

He kept flipping pages and reading as he spoke.

"Master, what's going on?"

He looked up from the notebook. "I was right about you, Gaultier."

"I don't understand –"

"The Queen is ready." He thrust the notebook towards me. "And so we must be."

"War?"

"I can't say for sure. All I know is he returned last night –"

"He?"

He frowned. "The man you were supposed to kill this morning."

Shit.

"Master... I –"

"That doesn't matter for now. You'll have a chance to redeem yourself. In the meantime, he's back and the Crown Council has been called up – the extended Council, that is."

"Who is he?"

"He's the man in the shadow."

I lost my breath for a second and bit back a croak. How did he know?

"I don't understand." I prayed he couldn't hear the fear in my voice.

"His name is Milton Ambreco. He's the Queen's Spymaster."

The... What?

"A summoning of the extended Crown Council hours after he returns in the middle of the night cannot be a coincidence," he continued as I tried to piece multiple streams of information into a coherent portrait. "He must have news that will drag us into war with the Empire."

Why would he...? The man had clearly turned his back on Queen Elisa and was feeding critical intelligence to the revolutionaries. Or had he instead infiltrated the Unsung Rebellion by pretending to be a traitor but was in fact a double agent? Did the master know this? And was that why he wanted him dead? Not likely. Master Callaghan kept a handful of unexpected traits hidden under his robes but a patriot he was not.

"Why did you ask me to kill him, Master?"

I regretted asking the question the second it left my lips. Obviously, if he'd wanted me to know he would have shared his motives this morning. Furthermore, I didn't *really* want to know. I just wanted to fade away like a thief in the night and leave this dark business behind.

"Why, so that he doesn't get to me first, of course."

***

THE COUNCIL ROOM STRUCK ME AS UNREASONABLY POMPOUS. During the past two hundred and seventy-three years that the Palace had stood in its current emplacement, overhanging the hamlet of Eastwharf from its perch on top of Torrindale's Mount (though the common folks called it Fat Glenda's Hill, after a popular, but portly, former monarch), the extended Crown Council had gathered here all of nineteen times, including five within a thirteen-day period when old King Allaster caught a bout of Serpent's Head Rabies one hundred and twenty-two years ago and the Baron of Rathmussen used his short-lived regency to show the world the Kingdom of Capnor still nursed imperial designs. In its otherwise limited incarnation, the Council met informally every fortnight in various locations suited to its member's needs and preferences, currently the Queen's own dining room. I was directed to a row of small wooden chairs set aside for observers along the western wall, while the master took his own seat at the U-shaped conference table between the Lord of Armouries and the City Administrator. Away from his laboratory, he looked quite uncomfortable being involved in affairs of state. A dozen or more long iron poles protruded high up near the ceiling from each of the four walls, proudly displaying the banners of the various arms of the monarchy from the Navy to the Cavalry to the Royal Family itself. There were far more participants than there were banners.

"All will be quiet," the Lord Chamberlain called the meeting to order after a few minutes of disorderly discussion had likely raised the collective level of speculation to its peak. He clapped his hands loudly three times and everyone at the conference table raised to their feet. I followed suit, largely unaware of the ceremonial script. Queen Elisa of House Barrettmoore, sovereign of the independent Kingdom of Capnor, entered the room at a hasty pace, without the boisterous fanfare that usually precedes or follows her in and out of the Throne Room. I'd never seen her so close or without a panache covering her dark hair shortly cropped to frame her visage. I reckoned these were perilous times indeed. The man in the shadow, who I now knew as Milton Ambreco, was walking at her side, taking one long stride for every two or three she did. His eyes didn't stray from his designated seat at the head of the conference table, next to the Queen's, though he undoubtedly felt the heat from all the longing stares locked in his direction, heard the silent acrimony coming from a roomful of men who, according to the master, envied with rage the many privileges he had carved for himself within the Queen's entourage.

"The extended Crown Council is now in session," the Lord Chamberlain said after the Queen gave him the expected nod. She sat first, followed by the rest of the assembly except for Milton Ambreco and the Lord Chamberlain. "I will not waste any time with formalities but rather go on with the order of business. We will first hear an extraordinary report from the Spymaster."

All eyes turned, once again, to Milton Ambreco as he took several seconds to look at each council member anxiously awaiting the latest intelligence from the continent. He didn't see me, though I expected he knew I'd be attending.

"As you may know all too well, the threat of invasion from across the Blue Sea of Karus has not been assessed as credible for at least a hundred years. I'm not here to tell you otherwise. It remains inconceivable that warships in sufficient numbers to constitute a landing threat would go undetected by dragon-mounted patrols. That being said, there are many in the imperial administration, including Emperor Malcolms himself, who continue to harbour fierce resentment towards us for the humiliation suffered by Prince Arturo" – he quickly glanced at the Queen, who smiled coyly – "after the so-called *White Geneva* affair unfolded."

"When's the extraordinary report you promised scheduled for?" a voice I couldn't readily identify asked, prompting a few timid chuckles amongst the assembly.

"Silence!" the Lord Chamberlain intervened.

"No, the Harbourmaster is quite right, my Lord," Milton Ambreco responded. "Much of the situation as you knew it yesterday is unchanged, except for this fact: over the past year, the Imperial Court in Dravengoth has commissioned secret submissions from the sharpest minds it could find in all relevant fields: engineering, metalworks, beast handling, alchemy, sorcery…"

The room started to simmer in hushed murmurs.

"Silence!" the Lord Chamberlain banged his open palm three times against the table. "Silence, we will have order!"

"The last of the wizards were exterminated during the Great Debacle over 300 years ago. What are you insinuating, Spymaster?" the Lord of Cavalry asked over the rabble, which suddenly died as the entire extended Council turned to the head of the table to hear Milton Ambreco's answer.

"My Lord, I am *insinuating* nothing at all. I stand here to inform the Council about a rival's intentions and capabilities based on information obtained by my operatives from several reliable sources, as required by my appointment. Any inference you or any member of the Council may draw regarding whether magic practitioners have returned to this world is out of my hands."

"So, this could be misinformation fed to your informants."

"I fail to see what this would accomplish. We are not a threat to the Empire, rather the opposite, in fact."

"But you acknowledge the possibility this intelligence could be –"

"My Lord, if you please," Queen Elisa interjected. "I would very much like to hear the end of this report."

The Lord of Cavalry, visibly miffed, conceded the floor with a short spread of his open palms and leaned back into his seat. Too bad, I thought. If wizards were back on the continent, I'd love to know where I could find one.

"The Spymaster will please resume," the Lord Chamberlain said. "Council members will refrain from interrupting the session."

Milton Ambreco appeared to be collecting his thoughts for a moment. "Thank you, my Lord. I was just relating our findings that the Imperial Court has covertly been seeking novel thought into potential means to coerce the Kingdom of Capnor into the fold of the Empire... including the use of sorcery. It would appear one of the latter proposals caught the eye of the Emperor. Unfortunately, our assets were unable to obtain full details of the plan's objectives and deployment, though they were able to learn it requires the acquisition of the Blue Gemstone of Karus."

All eyes turned to the Queen's neckline, disappointed to see she was wearing a different pendant.

"This plan sparked enough interest for the Emperor himself to authorise a covert incursion onto the island by a small squad of highly trained specialists in order to steal the Gemstone and return it to Dravengoth, where its power will be exploited by magical means and turned against us."

***

AIDA LOOKED AT ME AS IF I'D GONE COMPLETELY INSANE.

"I can't run away, Christopher. This is... Where would we go?"

A reasonable voice in my head insisted expediency had to be the primary factor driving my escape plan but I'd recently accepted Aida was the one person I couldn't lie to. On the other hand, having spared the time to fuck her twice before stating I had to run for my life and wished her to come along had severely dulled any hint of urgency I'd hoped to convey. "I haven't figured it out yet, but I know lots of places where we could blend in. I travelled a lot before I came here and –"

"No! Maybe you have the luxury of packing up and finding a new patron to house and feed you, but I don't. This is the only place I know. I'm nothing outside of the Palace."

"Don't you ever say that! There is so much more you can do than clean after the master. And you'll have me, I can teach you how to read and... I'll take care of you. Maybe... maybe we can marry."

She smiled like an old maid, with her fierce honey brown eyes fluttering beneath the starlight, being courted on the first day of spring by a green boy enjoying his first night out on the town. "Oh, Christopher... I'm not the kind of girl you want to marry."

She was wrong. It may have been accurate to think that someone of my standing was unlikely to marry someone of hers, but social convention would be the least of our troubles once the Council got their hands on a couple vials of Scorched Vine and foolishly uncorked its deadly spores. Maybe not today and most certainly not here, but I did want to marry her. The thought may have been utterly risible a month ago – hell, make that a week ago – but standing on the edge of the abyss has the sobering effect of sorting lust from love. I wanted to tell her we'd find a little country house by the side of a stream and raise a flock of sheep. Or maybe we could hide in plain sight, open an apothecary store in a bustling frontier town on the far end of the Empire. I would slip quietly out of bed every morning to go pick wildflowers from the fields and gently rouse her from sleep with the sweet aroma of jams and fresh coffee.

I delivered a quick kiss to her forehead. "I disagree but we can argue that later," I said. "We need to get far away from here. This place is doomed… and maybe the Empire is doomed as well, but I know that if we stay here, we won't stand a chance."

She pulled up the cotton sheet to cover her silky white breasts and took my left hand into her right. "Christopher, I am not going anywhere until you tell me what's going on."

The proceedings of the Council session were obviously not meant to be repeated outside the room but, in all likelihood, half the Palace would be buzzing with rumours of war by the morning. If I had any chance of convincing her to run away tonight, she needed to know that I trusted her with the truth, no matter how grim and dire. So I told her of Milton Ambreco's revelations to the Council and of the plan to allow the thieves access to the Palace and let them steal a fake Gemstone to bring back to Dravengoth. She questioned the wisdom of letting them come and go. Even with a fake prize, she argued, surely they'd be able to report useful information about the city's defences or the Palace's vulnerability. Where was the payoff?

"That's where I come in," I said with gravity.

"You?"

"Well, it's actually the master's plan but… Alright, let me start from the beginning. Years ago, the Queen instructed the Council to develop a weapon so terribly frightening no part of the Empire would ever again consider rattling sabres within earshot of our envoys across the sea. She would even settle for something that didn't work. As long as it was plausible and convincing enough, it wouldn't actually need to be used."

"What was it?"

"At first, they called it the *Black Cyclop*. It was a contraption that would shoot a beam of superheated steam above a village or a city or a military camp, anywhere we can bring it, and turn the clouds into fine flakes of ash that would rain down upon the target and make anyone within 10 miles who inhaled any of it drop dead like exhausted donkeys."

She was unimpressed. "That sounds like horseshit."

"It does, doesn't it?" She giggled. "Well, you'll be glad to know we drew blueprints, and even built a couple of prototypes to encourage any enemy spy lying around to report they had actually seen this doomsday device. I think some powdered wig in the Admiralty also talked about poisoning an entire village and spreading the rumour it was the work of the Cyclop, but they never really got around to it."

"That's a lovely story, Christopher," she said, her voice heavy with sarcasm, "but it's almost curfew in the servants quarters and I'm still waiting to hear why you want me to sneak out in the middle of the night and leave the island."

Right.

"Well, the master wasn't quite satisfied with the end result, and you know as well as I do how the master likes to please the Queen" – she rolled her eyes and sighed – "so he reckoned the idea of a machine manufacturing a plague was missing the mark... but not by much. There was another way, a much easier way in fact. Instead of zapping a cloud to grind it into nasty plague powder, all he needed to do was zap people with an actual plague vector that he would concoct right here in his laboratory. The trick was to make that vector a living organism, so it could jump from one person to the next. Then all he had to do to decimate a whole city was infect two or three well-targeted social butterflies and let his weapon handle the rest."

Aida had never been instructed in anything formal other than cleaning garments and bed sheets for the wretched parasites who claimed her servitude as their birth right, but she was a lot smarter than most of them. "They're going to steal the fake gemstone, but bring home the plague with them…" She was horrified. "Christopher, what did you do?"

"I didn't know any of this until it was too late, I swear!"

That much was true. The master had first asked me to track down old accounts of possible mass infections: figure out how they started, how they spread, how people died. So much of it was unreliable, mostly oral testimony transcribed on scrolls years after the fact, or often second or third hand descriptions from dodgy history books. I thought we were getting prepared to stave off an incoming wave, that maybe there had been quiet rumours from across the sea about people suddenly dying of a mysterious disease. This was an epic struggle I was ready for: man harnessing science and forgotten knowledge against an existential threat simmering deep within the bowels of nature. I thought we were serving the common good. I was wrong.

At that moment I thought I'd lost her. She looked at me the way a disappointed mother looks at a child who just killed a kitten, and our age difference suddenly felt real, almost embarrassing.

"You have to make this right," she whispered.

"I know," I said, though, despite years spent learning arcane secrets and pondering upon the meaning of life, I had no idea how to undo the terrible mistake that lay dormant in my laboratory.

There was an insistent knock at the door. We both perked up from the pull of despair and she mouthed 'Who is that?' while pulling the sheets up to her neck. I put on a robe while the caller knocked again and asked through the closed door who was there.

"Gaultier! Now!" Milton Ambreco hissed from the other side.

Shit.

Aida wrapped herself in the bedsheet and ran to hide in the wardrobe closet, while I clumsily tried to comb my hair with wet fingers.

"Open the damn door!"

I made sure there were no obvious signs I had company and opened up. "Sorry, I wasn't expecting you. Please, come in." The quarters I'd been assigned were not meant to entertain but I did keep a small desk and sitting stool underneath the only window. I gestured for him to sit down and he appeared to regain some of his usual composure.

"I believe we have a few important items of discussion ahead of us."

"Don't you think maybe it's unwise to..." I didn't want Aida to find out this way about my side-line episode with the revolutionaries, but I reckoned that horse was at least a league or two out of the barn by now. "After your little speech this morning, I figured we wouldn't –"

"No, here will do, and now." He waited for me to sit as well but soon realised the only spot available was the unmade bed. He went on. "I'm sure you can imagine my surprise this afternoon when Master Callaghan reported to the Council" – his tone and demeanour changed dramatically – "that you weren't entirely forthcoming with my colleague this morning!"

He got on his feet and poked a surprisingly hard index finger on my sternum. "Do you think this is a friendly game of chess? Or maybe you reckon you're the first clever lad I've met and that you'll be pulling my strings in no time, is that it?"

"No," I whispered.

"Perhaps I did not make this clear, but," he said softly, "whatever it is you think you're doing, I am much, *much* better at it than you."

I could hardly breathe. He reverted back to a more casual posture.

"I understand your conversion to the cause was not, shall we say, entirely genuine. I've been in this trade a long many years and many of my best informants would have gladly dropped me down in the middle of the sea locked up in an iron cage, as would you, I have no doubt. The difference between you and them is that, whatever their motivations might have been, whatever disdain they nurtured deep in their heart, they all learned never to lie to me. You would be wise to follow their lead. If you don't already despise me, I'm confident you will soon. Pretending this situation is pleasant for either of us is unproductive. Trying to resist it is pointless."

We stared defiantly at each other for a few seconds. I could think of nothing to say that wouldn't make things worse. I swallowed. "What do you want from me?"

He sat back down on the stool. "The fake Gemstone will be just that, nothing more, nothing less."

"What? Why?"

"There is no need to decimate the Empire just yet. All in due time, which is why you will complete the weapon nevertheless, but you will deliver it to me. I want the recipe and a sample. Actually, make that several samples."

"And what happens then?"

"Then we continue our friendly game of –"

Aida sneezed. He slowly turned towards the wardrobe, and then back towards me with a playful smile on his face.

"Is there someone hiding in there?" he asked.

"No," I said. "That was just the wood creaking. It does it all the time."

"Try again."

I looked around the room. There had to be some heavy or sharp object to hit him with. Maybe a pen? No, that wouldn't do. I needed something that – what in the name of Karus? He was on his feet, dramatically tiptoeing his way to the closet, shushing me with a finger to his lips like a thief in a children's stage play.

"Don't open –"

He opened it without any concern that whoever in there could fling a club or a dagger at him. Of course, he found Master Callaghan's personal servant standing amongst my garb, with a bed sheet wrapped around her naked body. "M'lady," he said, extending his arm to help her step out.

***

I LET GO OF THE GAROTTE AND RAN TO THE CORNER TO RETCH. Kneeling on the stone floor, I could taste desperation mixing up with the bile rushing up from my entrails and felt relief, because killing a man shouldn't have been that easy. Although the discovery of the body, slumped in a chair with his head flung backwards and purple marks across his neck, wouldn't shock anyone who knew anything of the intrigues going on in the Palace, the sight was still revolting. At least, to me it was. I'd come here hoping to make him see he was marching all of us to our doom. Before the deed, standing at the door with sweaty hands and a cheap leather string carefully rolled up in the front pocket of my britches, all I could think of was his lust for inflicting needless pain and decided he was a despicable creature at the best of times, incapable of redemption, I was certain of that. I'd walked in the room knowing my hands would be stained with blood before I walked out again, and the only hope that remained then was that he wouldn't beg me for his life before it was done.

"I'm sorry, Master. It was the only way."

Milton Ambreco had left shortly after finding Aida in the closet. He'd not said another word, but nevertheless managed to convey the only message that mattered on his way out. *I got you by the balls, boyo!*

Aida and I looked at each other for a long time after he left, also in silence. Now she knew what I knew and understood neither of us could stick around much longer. In a way, Milton Ambreco had been much more persuasive than I could have ever hoped to be, but we finally agreed there was one extra job left to do before we disappeared.

I'll do it, she'd offered, as if we'd been speaking of buying a few apples at the market for a pie. She mentioned the way Ambreco looked at her nakedness, and how easily she could get into his britches. She'd bring another serving girl along, Fiona perhaps, with smooth burgundy lips to keep his cock occupied and his mind distracted while she slit his throat. I should have stepped in and told her the man was a vicious viper, that it was too dangerous, or simply that it was a man's job. But there were already several reasons I wasn't a knight, and I wasn't above adding another one to the list. Moreover, I'd have a task of my own. The master had seen all my notes. It would take him a week at most to complete the work even if I burned them. That loose end had to be tied up before anything else.

He'd heard me walking in, told me to go fetch him some breakfast, muttered something about Aida having her moonblood. A couple of crates filled with leather-bound treatises lay in front of his writing desk, where he was sitting and poring over one of them. I told him we had to destroy the Scorched Vine notes before it got out of our control and everyone was dead, though I already knew what he would say.

Nonsense, Gaultier! We've been fighting a silent war with the Empire for three hundred years, and now you'd have us throw away the ultimate weapon, on the brink of victory?

We weren't at war, I argued. To be sure, we were stuck in a historical pattern wherein successive rulers on both shores of the Blue Sea of Karus distrusted each other for institutional reasons that defied any actual evidence of ill intentions. But we weren't at war. Wasn't it ironic that I'd have to kill him for denying my understanding of the world after he'd taught me almost everything I knew?

Master, I said, *we've gone too far. You can extrapolate the data as well as I do. We won't be able to contain it. It won't burn itself out until it's claimed every living soul. You have to agree this is madness!*

He stood up, never taking his eyes off me, and walked over to a locked cabinet where I knew he kept a bottle of Sherry tucked away behind a tight row of dark green ceramic jars. He poured half a glass and drank it in a single sip.

Would you like some? he asked, and without waiting for an answer hurled the bottle in my direction. It missed me by an arm length and smashed against the wall on my left in a small explosion of stale liquor and shattered glass. *No! Not this time! For every day Capnor maintains its independence from the Empire, Ambreco gets the glory. But not this time. This victory will be mine, and I'll be damned if you, or anyone else, takes it away from me!*

I'd seen him act this way before, like an enraged beast whenever word of bizarre misfortune afflicting the Empire raced through the Palace like wildfire, and questioned each time where his allegiance secretly rested. But now, after the previous day's impromptu assassination attempt and glorious revelation of our impending success before the Crown Council, I understood he wasn't a traitor. He was jealous of the man who kept the enemy reeling.

What's he done to you, Master?

He'd trudged back to the desk and slumped in the chair, exhausted and angered by the memories.

I was handsome, once, you know, he said. *Just like him.*

No... there was no way the master was ready to risk killing everyone alive on the account of his rival's good looks, was there? It sounded ridiculous but the candlelight reflecting in his eyes could have been dancing to the rhythm of the mad calculus rushing inside his mind.

How can she let him share her bed? She's the Queen and... he's just a filthy worm!

Well, that was interesting: Milton Ambreco, Spymaster, revolutionary, double agent and Paragon of Wickedness at large, also fucked Her Majesty the Queen of Capnor in his spare time. It occurred to me finding a more deviant man would have been a heavy task, and I wondered whether Aida had already killed him.

The master had started to sob like a sad pup. I'd moved quietly behind him and did what I'd come here to do.

***

I WALKED OUT OF THE LABORATORY AND ROAMED the empty halls longer than I should have, hoping to catch Aida dragging a heavy bag around the corner and smiling a murderous grin. Instead, I ended up wandering into the kitchen and reckoned I should have pocketed more Nakrofix while I was on a roll, but all I could spot keeping warm on the stove were black sausages and diced potatoes. Turns out I wasn't such a bad assassin after all. If only I hadn't botched my first assignment... well, maybe not. Things might have been worse, in fact. The Queen may have declared open war and, instead of leading the Emperor's stealthy squad to a fake Gemstone, the Council would be making plans for dragon-riders to carry the plague to the four corners of the Empire. At least now I had time to breathe and plot while the Council congratulated its collective wit.

I needed to head back and finish packing. We should try to make it onto a fast-moving ship before anyone discovered the master's body, though with Aida and myself on the run, it may be days before anyone else found their way to the laboratory. Maybe I could plant some clues to suggest I'd been killed as well, or elsewise taken. The Council would have to conclude the Spymaster had been fed misinformation and question everything else they thought they knew about the Empire. One way or another, I couldn't stop the impending war, but at least I could ensure it'd be the traditional kind. Maybe the Queen would even send her own commando to get me back and the precious research stored in my head.

Damn! The research – I'd left all the notebooks in the master's laboratory. Though I was sure no one else could make sense of it now, this was the one loose end that absolutely needed to be closed. Otherwise, this whole perverse game of charades would be in vain.

I ran the last hundred yards, confident nobody would be around to see me break down almost in panic, though ready to silence the first poor sap who'd make the mistake of looking at me the wrong way with a brick to the side of the head. Out of breath, I dropped to my knees in the doorway. The body was gone!

Shit! Had I fucked this up as well? No, he was dead! I'd heard his life whistle out of him and left him slumped in the chair... He'd struggled and squirmed and writhed until he didn't. And I'd kept pulling for another minute at least, just to make sure... No, someone had moved him while I was upstairs... someone... who? Maybe Aida? Yes! She must have come back to find me here and saw the body and... took the notebooks? Would she have known what to look for? They'd been stacked, all five of them, on the shelf by the door. I should have burned them immediately. Should have, couldn't, didn't. Somehow, I thought, I could turn it on its head and use the research to prevent infection next time the Great Mother decided she'd seen enough of us.

Damn it! It had to be *him*. Which meant... I had to find Aida!

I ran all the way this time back to my quarters. The door was slightly ajar.

"Aida?" I called out. "Are you here?"

Silence.

"Aida?" I pushed the door open with the tips of two fingers, peeked inside. A naked body lay sprawled on the bed.

No!

I rushed to the bedside and breathed a sigh of relief. It was only Fiona, the redhead serving girl who was supposed to create a diversion. Her hands were tied with twine to the bed frame above her head and she was pinned to the mattress by a long silver dagger rammed through her mouth. Her bright eyes still screamed in terror and, as if that message wasn't clear enough, a short note scrawled on a piece of parchment had been carefully placed atop her nether regions. I already knew what it said but grabbed and read it nevertheless.

As a result of his recent demise, I took the liberty to re-assign Callaghan's wench to my personal service. If you know what's good for her (and I believe you do), you'll get me what I asked for and stop playing games. As an incentive for you to deliver promptly, know that I'll be teaching her new tricks until you're done.

I stumbled down to the floor and buried my face in my hands. There was only one thing left to do. The filthy bastard really did hold me by the balls.

***

COMPLETING THE LAST LEG TURNED OUT TO BE FAR SIMPLER than I'd expected. Three days of searing pain and sweat meant nothing in order to save the woman I loved from the throngs of a sociopath, as long as I ignored the inconvenient fact that the fruit of that labour would in turn wipe out humanity before the end of harvest season. It was an irrational trade-off I couldn't reconcile at all with any of the values or principles that had brought me to this point, but I reckoned I'd go insane if I tried to take in the larger picture. I needed to keep Aida alive, one step at a time, even if I knew exactly where this path led. Fortunately, the scientific light in my brain hadn't gone completely dormant. In fact, I found it a lot easier to fool the emotional blob I'd been reduced to, and lay down the foundations for one last scheme, than willfully ignore the inevitable perils of abetting Milton Ambreco. Odds were, he would hack me into pieces before I knew whether I'd pulled it off but, again, I'd worry about that once my neck was on the chopping block.

I'd gambled our last hope on the reliability of a stable boy who I knew picked up a couple crates of fresh apples from the harbour every other day.

He could usually be bribed to leave one or two wrapped in cloth napkins outside my door every once in a while but smuggling a message out of the palace proved to be more costly. Even with the few silver coins I managed to scrape out of a locked box hidden in the master's privy, I was surprised to find out negotiation is an underrated art in this day and age. The plan also hinged a great deal upon luck. I'd been stuffed in a barrel when taken in and out of the Unsung Rebellion's lair down by the harbour. And since I couldn't exactly instruct the stable boy to track down which of the waterfront's several whorehouses doubled as a secret den of revolution, I'd had to pick all of them. Six identical messages went out yesterday morning, warning the revolutionaries that Milton Ambreco had lost his marbles and was about to release Master Callaghan's 'living poison' into the city. It was imperative they prevent anyone – at any cost – from entering or leaving the Palace for at least three weeks and should seal the gates from the outside. I would do what had to be done from the inside.

I tied up my notebooks into a neat stack with a leather string -- the same one I'd used to strangle the master, incidentally -- and placed it on top of a wooden case that contained six vials of the colourless, odourless and formless poison I'd finally perfected 12 hours before. They appeared empty, which I thought added a sweet touch of serendipity to the matter. It might just prompt the Spymaster to accuse me of thinking him a fool and open one of them to prove his point. That would suit my purpose just fine and spare me the trouble of having to remove lucky number seven from the inside of my sleeve, unseen, and smash it at his feet. I added the fake Gemstone to this odd care package and walked out of my laboratory without locking the door behind me. I doubted I'd be back.

Survival instinct didn't kick in until I was a floor below his apartments. Who said I had to sacrifice everything just to stem a nasty bout of coughing going around the Empire? I was young, relatively healthy... maybe I could beat it? Let it run its course and... maybe I'd built an immunity by virtue of small dose exposure? I could kick the door in and smash the vial in the middle of the room while grabbing Aida by the hand and... Damn, why didn't I think of making a couple of smoke bombs while I was at it?

I took a deep breath.

This was no time for heroics. I'd spent three days thinking it over from every possible angle. Enough already! There was only one way to stop this madman, and it had to be done now. I climbed up the last flight of stairs and announced myself to the large sentinel blocking the entrance to the suite.

"I had a feeling today would be the day," Milton Ambreco said without lifting his eyes from a fat report he was engrossed in. "How many vials are in the case?"

"Six."

"Good work."

"One will be enough."

"Redundancy is key in my profession."

"But you'll only ever get to use one."

He looked up at me. "Gaultier, I'm starting to like you. Don't start this argument again."

"I'll keep making this argument until you understand there is no hiding from this plague. Whatever pain you think you can impose on the enemy I guarantee you'll suffer tenfold as a result."

I could tell he wasn't interested. "That's enough. Leave all of that with me and get out of my sight."

I hesitated. Maybe I still had a chance.

"Aida's coming with me," I said without much conviction.

He smiled and dropped the report back on the desk. "Actually, I've been enjoying your wench," he said, "and I think I'll keep her for a while longer if that's all the same to you. Now get out."

I reached inside my sleeve and grabbed the seventh vial from its hidden pocket while he turned his back, my presence forgotten as he returned his attention to his document. I reckoned he wouldn't hesitate to slay me on the spot this time, so I looked for a sign of Aida's presence, anything to focus on during my last few seconds of consciousness. Nothing. I couldn't wait any longer and told myself she'd understand.

I raised my arm to throw the vial, hesitating just long enough for a giant, hairy fist to reach out from behind and cover my hand like molten caramel coating around a candy apple. The guard grunted in short bursts while his other arm wrapped around my neck.

"What's this, Gaultier? More games?" Milton Ambreco said before standing up in exasperation. "I was told you were smart."

He pointed at my hand with a curt nod. The guard released his grip just enough for his boss to force open my palm and grab the glass vial between his thumb and index finger, intact and apparently empty. He looked at it for several seconds and understood what I'd been about to do.

"I suppose you thought that'd be pretty ironic, didn't you," he said. "Poetic, even. How would that go, I wonder? Let's see, 'In the end, the mad king was felled by the very same object he'd sought as a means to destroy everything that stood in the way of his vision.' Is that what you had in mind?"

There was the smug face I'd expected to scorn at me back in that dank basement a few mornings ago, the deceptively handsome face of a thug who had mistakenly thought good luck lasts forever.

"You're scum," I said, grinning. Maybe I wouldn't kill him today, but he would eventually kill himself with the toy I'd manufactured for his amusement, along with the rest of the world. As regretful as that was, he'd just taken away the last card hidden up my sleeve. But quite frankly, I no longer cared.

He spat in my face. "Get rid of him."

Shit! That's what I should have done. I tried to pool as much saliva as I could, but the guard was already pivoting me back towards the hallway. I started to wriggle, trying to get free of the brute's violent embrace, but his grip remained as firm as ever. The door to the bedroom opened suddenly and my love appeared, glowing in sunlight from the open window behind her.

"Don't kill him! You promised he'd live."

"Shut up and get back in there!" Milton Ambreco bellowed.

The brief exchange allowed for a quick distraction. I launched myself to the left with the intention of creating enough dead weight to force my captor into a little dance. He stumbled to one knee trying to maintain his hold on my arms and I managed a feeble kick to his stomach. He let go. I ran to Aida, cupped my hands around her face and kissed her salty lips as if tomorrow might never come. The guard, already back on his feet, grabbed the back of my neck and yanked me away.

"I'm sorry, my love!"

Out in the hallway, I could hear her yell sharp little shards of profanity and fight the Spymaster trying to restrain her best he could.

"Shut up, you stupid bitch! Get in there and I'll show you what it feels like to be fucked by a real man."

I didn't dare imagine what he was about to do to her. My only solace came from the thought that I'd found the courage to open the eighth vial and infect myself with Scorched Vine this morning before leaving the laboratory. Now that Aida was too, I was curious how long it would take for the Queen to become sick.

To Kill A God

By Marren MacAdam

THE HALLS OF THE GODS STILL GLISTENED amongst the infinite suns and moons in the sky, even if the lights of those who inhabited these halls faded. How to describe the architecture of every style and type of peoples that once populated the Earth? The ever-shifting structure, on this day, settled on impossibly tall white marble, motifs for each and every of the gods and their stories wrapping around the stonework like vines, as beautiful stained glass lined the walls. Light spilled eternal from these halls, like a glowing beacon, and while Tyr did not notice, one window had gone dark.

The chatter of the halls was like a flock of sparrows arguing, indistinct and scattered. Tyr's footsteps echoed throughout the hall, bringing some semblance of order back to it. The stately cobblestone beneath his feet seemed to shift before him, straightening itself out, dust disappearing before his feet even touched it, as if afraid to displease him. Silence followed his ascent to the higher chairs and tables on the dias at the end of the hall.

Eyes fell on him, and what was once chatter turned to whispers.

Tyr still remembered the days when all this seemed impossible. On the one side sat Mercury and Ganesha, the former growing softer and rounder as the years passed by, yet still with eyes as sharp as a blade; the latter seemed thinner by the day, the once joyous physique dwindling. Tyr's jaw tightened, gritting his teeth. *We are dying.*

Flanked by the clamour-turned-silenced that surrounded Tyr, he approached the central dias at the end of the hall. The chair sat alone, a simple shaped high back iron chair. In the shining metal of the chair, Tyr caught a look at his face: it was drawn in more than it had once been, leanness turned into a kind of old age, where skin clings to bones and fat fades. His once long and deep dark hair now grayed, his beard a salt and pepper mess. If his jaw was not already set, it was now. A grim reminder of what the loss of humanity's faith and presence on the Earth had wrought upon him and his siblings: mortality.

Tyr sat, facing the hall filled with thousands of gods in varying degrees of decay. The Scourge did not take them all equally: those who were older died first, the all fathers and mothers, some of the younger, weaker ones also perishing. There were theories on why it seemed to affect certain gods more than others, some quicker than others, but it did not matter much to them. After the first century without humanity, the gods were a pack of crumbling ruins, and one did not compare degrees of destitution.

As Tyr took his seat, the tranquility that his ascent brought was crushed under a wave of voices, all in panic, raised to the rafters themselves. Tyr allowed the chaos its place, letting the gods have their emotions, before responding with a booming growl that came from deep within his throat.

Silence. His ghost hand itched, the stump now resting against his face. The constant reminder of the price of a promise.

Tyr was not a god to revel in drama, but as Elected he had to give his fellows their performance. He sat, awaiting a singular voice daring enough to report what in the gods realm had happened.

From the silence came a single voice, nondescript in gender, fluctuating between heights of mountains and lows of valleys, yet a presence known well by Tyr. Loki approached the dias, their ever shifting form settling on a womanly form, hips swaying at their approach. Tyr grumbled, but gave his sibling the floor to speak nonetheless.

For all of Tyr's lack of interest in the aesthetics of presentation, Loki made up for their sibling. They turned, their cloak a fluttering presence behind them, like wings of a black bird, stretching out to welcome the eyes falling upon them. They spoke, clearly above the din that started. "Siblings gathered here, in our most sacred of halls and in our darkest hours, I come bringing terribly dire news. This morning, upon my daily walk, I heard an awful scream that pierced through my thoughts. Rushing as fast I could, I made my way towards the sound only to be… Too late. I found our dearest sister, beautiful Aphrodite, dead, her blood still pooling in the stonework."

They paused, allowing the gravity to sink in. The Hall was silent.

"After what felt like a millenia, I roused the Gods Wardens. Guan Yu arrived first, and after taking in the scene himself, we called the assembly here. At this time," they turned back now to Tyr, bowing low, "We do not have any particular leads."

The proclamation echoed throughout the hall, and the cacophony of concern rose once more. Tyr mused to himself, taking the scene in, *did we always bicker like dogs before a meal, our tails between our legs like whelps? An ounce of the mortality humanity faced and we became worse than their darkest.*

Rising from his chair, the chattering of the sparrows stopped once more. Tyr could feel the weight of their fears on him, their anxieties in the room striking him like waves of enemies upon a shield. It was heavy. "Siblings, I call upon you to bring dignity upon yourselves and these halls. We will not cower from these insidious shadows that work amongst us, cowardly as they are to strike one of us alone. I will not preach to you that we are dying: that the loss of humanity, their leaving of Earth as a heaving, rotting mess, has left us weakened. Yet to abuse this, to *accelerate* a process so foreign to us... Is sickening. What could one gain from the senseless murder of an already dying race?

"I assume full cooperation by any that I approach. As Elected, I am tasked with the terrible burden of uncovering this unprecedented crime. Do not allow yourself to be alone, stay in pairs at the very least. We cannot let our sister be the first on a list of the dead."

Signaling the end of the meeting, Tyr stepped down from the dias to leave once more. The whispers that rose around him did not quiet upon his approach. Their fear was palpable. *Who, or what, could kill a god? Even a weakened one? And for what reasons would one of our siblings take another's life...*

***

TYR WALKED THE NEVER ENDING GARDENS, mulling over the events of the morning. He tensed and loosened his hand, rhythmically, as he fretted over the information. To call the Halls afterwards solemn would be an understatement: they had taken on the thick air of a funeral. The Gardens, however, allowed Tyr a moment to himself, to collect himself away from others. The receptive nature of the Gardens, like much of the Halls, responded to his temperament: simple, hardy white flowers flanked him, trees of spruce and cedar giving their delicate, yet defiant nature solace in a high, winter sun. The cobblestones were orderly, flecked with the beginnings of winter snow, yet beneath this layer of snow was not a single patch of weeds or moss.

Pacing the Gardens, Tyr went over the possible suspects that came to mind. It was not simple to pinpoint the motive of why someone would assassinate such a high profile goddess as Aphrodite, especially with no apparent threat or demand left behind. While all the gods were weakened because of the lack of their humans' prayers, who now found gods in their far distant stars, Aphrodite was a popular one to the mortals even in their last days of faith: a goddess of love, beauty, and joy, what mortal did not call out for these in their lives? Nor was she hated amongst her siblings in the years since the Departure: she often would act as mediator between feuding factions, bringing peace and serenity where she could.

As if by an old instinct, Loki came to mind. The Trickster god. How many great disturbances were laid at their feet? And yet… Tyr felt it could not be them. Loki was not the same god they once were since the Departure. They seemed hollow, lost at times. Something Tyr felt deeply. But they were never a god either to *murder* for a jest.

Perhaps a jealous god? A rival in her domain? Freya was a possibility, but this didn't really feel like her work. Freya would rather challenge a god to a duel than assassinate them in the night. Besides, the two were close after the Union of all the gods. Hades, possibly, with his eternal frustrations with his fellows.

As if an answer to his question, Hades walked by in the distance. His arm entwined with Persephone, the path they left behind was a mixture of death and regrowth. He laughed, deep and echoing, while her footsteps seemed to barely touch the ground beneath them. *Unlikely, he has too much invested in her to throw that away on... What? What gain did our murderer even get?*

Frustration filled Tyr. He was angry at how little he knew of his fellow gods, their motives, now that they all seemed so stagnant.

Tyr felt their presence before they appeared to him. Loki brought with themself always a presence of change, a breath of fresh air, playfully teasing. Some of the once pristine, simple white flowers turned into multi coloured things, petals a rainbow of hues and sensations. The cobblestones rebelled, some crooked, others spotted with moss and weeds breaking through their cracks.

Tyr could already feel the tension in his neck building.

"Brother! I figured I would find you here. Always a consistent one, yes, that was always you, even in these dire times. You truly can be so easy to read, you know that yes?"

Tyr tensed, before greeting his sibling. "Loki. Have you any news?"

"Tsk, tsk, where are your manners? For such a principled one, you truly have *no sense* of social graces. You should spend more time with the gods of China, maybe they could teach you how to at least be a little welcoming. Maybe then you'd be less of an ugly, brutal leather glove and more... Well, really, anything." Loki smirked, having circled around Tyr now.

In this moment, Loki chose a comfortable persona, an androgynous look, donning a face that reflected equal parts masculine and feminine features, depending on the lighting. They were clean shaven in one moment, with their afternoon's stubble appearing in the next, cheeks at once full and plump, then angled and sharp. Ever shifting and confounding.

"You expect me to be polite to the one who brought such stress upon my dwindling life? Seriously, sibling, sometimes I wonder if you learned not from your " Tyr spoke.

"Not so much politeness, just basic respec-- To Hel with it, brother, you're impossible. No, I don't have any more information for you. If I did, I would have started with that." A sparring moment of seriousness crossing their face. It did not last, as Loki's usual grin returned, "Can't your dearest sibling be *worried* about you? I could swear I hear your teeth shattering upon my approach. I merely hoped to ease your anxieties."

"Leaving would do that quite well, actually."

"Prickly as ever, brother. I like that about you, y'know? You wouldn't know, but you should." Loki squatted down, inspecting one of the flowers of their creation. It refracted the light, like some polished gem. "So, who is on your List? I'm sure you have one, all neatly ordered, with many columns and rows, yes?"

"I have a few… But no, calling it orderly would be…" Tyr looked off, a storm brewing in his knitted brows.

"Ohh. It is bad then."

"Yes. I cannot make any reasonable sense of such a senseless murder. Who would cut short our already shortening lives? And for what purpose? I see no reason for it, nothing that would cause us to turn to such brutal measures."

"Ohh, you are always such an honourable one. *Likely* motives? Truly? The gods are wilting and dying around you and you still propose a *rational* culprit?" Loki spoke, half chiding, half genuine concern.

"What would you propose then, Trickster?"

"These are irrational times, brother. We are *dying*, mortals below. Why would you expect us all to act as stoically as you? Why would you suspect that none might act *drastically*."

"Strong claims, sibling. But I cannot chase fantasies of a grand plot without evidence for it. Why would I believe there's more afoot than a simple bout of anger or jealousy?"

Loki laid back on the railing, it changing form to be far more comfortable than the previous stonework of Tyr's devising. The flower twirled in their hands. "Mmmm mmm, fair, fair. Okay, so you need evidence then, eh? Well why don't we go and give a little visit to our dearly deceased?"

***

TYR DID NOT KNOW WHAT TO EXPECT as he made his way down the corridors of the Halls, what to steel himself against. He was familiar with death quite intimately; but this spoke of more. The Halls themselves made transit easy enough, as they readjusted themselves so that one did not need a map to find where they wanted to go. The god could simply will where they wanted to be, and the halls would respond.

Of course, that made it difficult to go somewhere someone did *not* want to be, yet needed to be. The odd silence of Loki, an unusual reverence about them, moved Tyr to act. It was not a time for cowardice, especially at a time when even a trickster god was without laughter.

Even dead, Aphrodite's room spoke of her soul through and through. Tyr knew that when a god died, their influence on their sacred sanctuary did not wilt away. Aphrodite's beauty infused itself in every aspect of the room, even in the morbid new light it was cast in. Her body lay atop the bed, deep red satins, with a lovely gold threading that highlighted dozens of scenes of lovemaking. Adorning her walls were beautiful paintings of many of the loveliest mortals across the millenia: they were the chosen of Aphrodite, and some say she even visited them at night to lay beside them. The room was filled with comfort and beauty in every crack, even as the pool of blood on the floor distracted from that.

That pool of blood seemed odd. It did not follow the cracks of the stonework underneath her bed. No, it seemed rather to form... Petals of a flower. Surely that was no accident. Yet why a flower?

As Tyr took in this information, he noticed more and more of this imagery of a flower. It was like the walls themselves moved, the forms of it taking on new spots across the walls, painted in the deep crimson blood that was once Aphrodite's godsblood.

Loki approached behind him, a slight audible gasp escaping their lips.

"Was it this way when you found her, sibling?" Tyr spoke.

"Ahhh it was... I hadn't noticed it all, of course. One doesn't find a goddess *dead* and take in the scenery, right? But what are... These?" Their eyes, usually a constant shifting mess, seemed hyper focused on the lines of the symbols. "Brother, I feel this may be more than just jealousy."

Tyr laughed, a short bark. "Quick thinking."

Loki's face, however, seemed a constipated knot of feelings and thoughts.

Tyr stood, taking in once more the room. There didn't seem to be any real forced entry he could spot. Of course, forced entry didn't really apply in the Halls. But neither did murder. He scanned the room, hoping for a hint at what could be.

Looking for a point of entry would be useless. One did not need to break into somewhere in the Halls. An open door policy was common, locks being a bygone concept. The gods had been at peace with one another for centuries before the Departure, and afterwards had solidified into a common identity of their newfound mortality.

Out of the corner of his eye, two things emerged as not part of Aphrodite's sanctuary itself, as intruders: a simple dagger whose metal seemed to both repulse and attract his attention, and a small, budding sapling in the pool of blood closest to the body of the goddess.

Tyr approached the first. The dagger, laying near the body in a not-so-subtle-way, was stained with the deep crimson that poured freely from the goddess, even now. The murder weapon. Yet it was left here, which raised more questions than answers. Then Tyr noticed the metal reflected the line strangely, a way he knew. *Is that godsmetal? I thought all the deposits of that cursed metal were destroyed in the Union.*

Godsmetal was, to put it simply, the only thing that could kill a god. It was a relatively nondescript-looking metal, a simple gray colour to it like beaten iron. Yet forged by the skilled smiths of the dwarves and it found an unholy purpose: it could puncture the gods flesh and spill their precious godsblood. It was universally condemned across all pantheons upon its discovery, as even the darkest of gods could not fathom to use it. It was known that each faction of the gods carried a few weapons made of the stuff, just in case, but that was a harsh reality of their cold wars. Tyr did not know if one needed to have godsmetal to kill a god in their current state, but he imagined that it was a surefire way to make sure the god stabbed did indeed die.

The metal rang like an awful, soft mosquito in his ears, and even Loki seemed perturbed by it.

"Is that…" They spoke, visibly shirking back from the cursed thing.

"Yes."

"Even in our current states, it never occurred to me that it might take that unhappy material to kill us. Better safe than sorry, I suppose, but still. It must have burned to hold it."

As Loki spoke, Tyr approached the small sapling. Squatting down, he came to a frightful realization: his knees did not creak under the movement. He reached out to the sapling with his good hand and noticed the veins seemed less visible, his complexion less sickly, his skin…

Oh mortals below.

The sapling called out, taunting in its simplicity, in its youth.

"Is that a damnable sapling, brother?" Loki's voice came from behind him.

Tyr grunted a reply, standing again to turn to his sibling.

"Brother… Do not take this poorly, but you look *far better* now. What in the nine realms…" Loki seemed flabbergasted, but then noticed their own body.

"Do you feel… younger too, sibling?"

"I do. And it feels *so very wrong.*"

"I do not like how this bodes, sibling. I feel we need to find anyone associated with these cursed plants."

"Do you mean…"

"Yes, surprisingly, she is a suspect now."

***

PACHAMAMA SAT AMONGST A DENSITY AND YOUTH of life that might have allowed one, for a split second, to forget that the gods were dying, if not that the tips of leaves were browning, new sprouts wilting and dying in

233

secluded corners before they could even reach the sun. The space was filled with verdant, lush hills and mountainscapes, the humidity a thick and heavy blanket of vitality. Pachamama sat amongst it like a glorious empress surrounded by her wondrous children. Her laughter left her throat, a layered symphony of thousands of different creatures calls, soft songbirds, musical bugs, and happy young.

In the presence of so much life, Tyr felt nauseated.

"Hail, brother Tyr! Bringer of order and rules. Mortals below, you know I did always struggle with that part. You will have to forgive me my manners and the state of my place, life tends to take over when you're not looking! And my children do so enjoy their unruliness. And who am I to deny my precious little ones such basic happiness?" Her smile was wide and kind, her voice like a babbling mother discussing her child's latest achievements. Tyr felt himself ease and his defenses lower.

"Ohh, no, but not today. No, today is no time for mirth and libations and celebrations. Today is a day for mourning, for the loss of our dear sister... And the darkness that grips at our roots like a hungry, savage beast." Her smile faded, tears flowing from her eyes like the purest of lakes. Around her, leaves that were once deep greens of life withered away, turning to crimsons, russets, and golds of autumn. The bright sunlight that poured endlessly from the sky darkened, clouds rolling in as a crisp, cool wind bit at their necks. Where once a mother's warmth resided, a barely-below-boil rage seemed to be.

Tyr stepped forward, clearing his throat, "Yes, I wish I came in times of life, mother. But I do not, sadly."

"Surely, yes. Questions, then, I presume? Please, sit, be welcome amongst my domain. The darker the night, the more important shelter and warmth amongst siblings is required, no? You too, Loki, I sense you lurking at the threshold! Come child, you know you are welcome here, too." She called out, a slight lightness to her tone returning.

Before her a simple stone table appeared, a bench of vines and wood on her side, which she laid upon comfortably, as two chairs for both Tyr and Loki rose. She gestured invitingly to the two, with Tyr grabbing his seat before Loki slinked out from the threshold. Loki took a feminine form now with wider hips and short, curly red hair atop their head, freckles dotting their pale skin.

"Know that we come here simply on a possible lead, this is not an accusation, mother." Tyr started, a rare bit of caution shown to the last of the parental gods. "We investigated the grisly scene just moments before arriving here. Evidence exists that, while not damning, points to you as having possible connection to the murder. Could you tell us where you were last night?"

To Pachamama's credit, she did not balk from Tyr's direct questioning. "Last night? I was at a dinner with a few of my partners. You know how cold these nights can be, and even in death it is welcome to lie with one another. No, I can say at the very least that I was quite… Occupied, last night."

Loki laughed, as Tyr's face turned a bright red.

"Ohhh, mother you are truly a treat sometimes! Mortals below, just to see Tyr go so beet red to realize that gods *fuck* regardless of their status!"

Pachamama chuckled, but her eyes remained fixed on Tyr.

"Right, of course. Unfortunately, those are all going to be gods I would assume to have a little more interest in preserving your innocence. Did you meet with anyone more neutral to you?" Tyr asked, trying to return the conversation, and his composure, to order.

"Ahhh Tyr, you always were such a rigorous one. Of course, that is a fair question. Fortunately for me, I suppose, I did find some company along my way home. Osiris, yes, that strange green skinned fellow. Never really talked with him much, you see, but he approached me in the Halls and well, you know I am never one to turn away company." She smiled at the last bit, before continuing.

"Yes, he offered to escort me to my room, what I assumed to be simply out of kindness, if not for the strange thing he said to me upon my arrival..."

Loki, who was previously finding the most unbearably unruly position to sit in their chair, eyed the mother goddess with extreme interest in that moment.

"Go on, mother," Tyr said.

"Well, see, he was telling me he was on his way to an arrangement of his, but he didn't allow me the time to fully ask him about it. I figured it was just some kind of game or possibly a meeting with a lover, who was I to judge there? But before he left, he bid me to stay safe in my room tonight... Which at the time, I didn't take to be much of anything. Just a simple well wishing?" Pacahamama spoke, uncertainty creeping into her voice.

Tyr grinned like a hungry wolf, leaning forward, his stare unbroken.

"Ahh well... Before he left, he motioned to give me something, a simple, folded piece of paper." She reached across the table to delicately lay it before the interrogating gods.

Tyr picked up the small paper, opening it up. Within the note was a simple image, to his immediate investigation possibly of minor magical properties. A simple, elegant flower like symbol constantly rotated through multiple phases of closing and opening up, going from a serene, closed bud to a lavish, unraveled bloom. The lines themselves were a basic magic, something even Tyr, who had no interest in magic, could have produced. It appeared to be something like a parlour trick, done for amusement or aesthetic purposes, but why Pachamama felt it was so dire eluded him.

"That one there, see, is the one that Osiris gave me before he took his departure. I have a matching note," which she revealed from her multicoloured dress, from a seemingly hidden pocket, before continuing, "which was originally given to me by another. *This* particular note matches that one identically, down to the shifting flower you can see. I did not join them, you must believe me on this: you know me, brother, for I am not one for groups. Too many rules and leaders and authority and *decisions*. Dreadful things. They get in the way of growth. But, I'm sure it has attracted... Others."

"Who gave you this note? The one who explained this 'group' you alluded to, mother?"

"Jesus Christ."

The two gods rose, Loki practically licking their lips at the implications, which Tyr shot down with a quick glance. The trickster all but cowered away from their siblings glare, but returned to a devilish grin once their brother turned back to address Pachamama.

"Thank you for answering our questions, Pachamama. Your answers have proved very helpful indeed. May the day find you some peace, for I feel it will not grant me that opportunity." He turned on his heels, his wolfskin cloak caught in the bitter wind that had taken over the once warm jungle. Loki gave an elaborate bow so deep that their curls fell loosely into their face.

"May justice find its way to these Halls, siblings. Please do not hesitate to reach out again, I will remain here for... Innocence's sake, shall we say?" Pacahamama called out to the retreating gods.

"Might be advisable, mother." Loki replied with a wink, turning to catch up with Tyr.

The two gods noticed, as steps from passing the threshold, that where once sprouts withered and died and leaves browned and aged, they now stood firm, filled with newfound vigor and life.

"Mortals below..." Tyr cursed, before crossing the threshold into the Halls proper.

***

Leaving the autumn colours behind them, Loki pulled up beside Tyr who walked with the purpose of an army. "Mortals below Tyr, what have we stepped into?"

As Tyr walked, the walls before him seemed barren, clean, as if burnt away by a raging fire that left nothing but stonework.

"Too much. Too many things, sibling. Symbols, poetry, hints, clues. I hate it. What does this blasted flower have to do with anything? With the death of a goddess?" Tyr growled, teeth bared as if his enemies were before him, waiting around the next corner.

"If only I had the answers, brother. While I do so enjoy tormenting you, this is well beyond me. I believe in tricks, not plots. Something about this stinks..." Loki's voice seemed to darken as they spoke, like their conspiratorial whispers might give the two away.

"I do not do well with these damnable affairs in the shadows, sibling. Where I cannot fathom their motives, their reasonings. The prayers I used to answer were so much… Clearer. But now that I find the call to justice being in my own hands I feel lost. This is not the battlefield I am prepared for."

"Things are different now, brother. You have to accept that things are not as clear and straightforward as they once were. You cannot keep pretending that we are as things were anymore," Loki responded, keeping step with Tyr. "You were elected to be *more* than this, more than just who you were but who we need you to be. The All Father…"

Tyr snapped his teeth like a wolf at the mention of Odin. He growled, primal-like.

Loki stood their ground, facing down Tyr's fury until it boiled away.

"You cannot keep doing that, brother. He is dead, as many of our elder gods are now. It awaits us all. And your constant embargo on so much as mentioning his name does *nothing* to change that fact. He charged you to be more than just your base self. Honour that."

Tyr sighed, his shoulders slumping. His footsteps stopped, and he leaned against the closest wall. The coolness of the stone against his back was bracing, and grounded him once more.

"I know, sibling."

Loki scoffed. "What? That's it? No apology? No thank you?

Mortals below, you never change do you?"

"No, I do not."

Compared to the gods before him, Jesus' room felt stark and barren. Simple, unadorned walls, with a small work space against the furthest wall. On the wall were carpentry tools, hammers, saws, chisels, and measuring apparatus'. On the table was a halfway assembled wooden stool, which Jesus turned around from to greet his visitors. He smiled slightly at the two, dusting his hands, covered in sawdust, on his apron before rising.

Of all the gods in the Halls, Jesus looked the most like the long lost mortals. Tyr was not a gaudy god by any means, but in the presence of Jesus he felt even his own aesthetics to be over the top and too bright. The face that greeted him was the ruddy colour of the deep, stained wood behind him; gray, kinked hair enhaloed him; his eyes burned with an endless fire.

"Welcome Tyr, god of justice! Welcome Loki, god of change. May you find yourself comfortable here." Jesus gestured before himself, as a simple wooden table and set of chairs appeared. Tyr did not immediately move to sit.

Unfazed, Jesus continued. "What brings the foreboding God of justice to dine at my simple table? To discuss the finer matters of our differences on that exact concept, perhaps? No, I see in your eyes, so cold and hostile, that you do not come to me with such mundane interests. Sadly. I do miss those days, brother."

Tyr strode forward, tossing the folded paper across the table to Jesus' side. Loki, now taking the form of a long haired, blond woman, eyes a startling green against alabaster skin, smiled like a tiger before its prey.

Jesus took the note, opening it, his once at ease smile dissolving from his face.

"So you know of this symbol, I take, *brother?*" Tyr spoke, like steel drawn from a scabbard. He would have no time for one who thought himself above or better than his equals.

"Mmm... Yes, I have seen it. It brings me no joy to admit that, nor to say I may... Know more about it then I am comfortable with." Jesus sat, turning the paper over in his hands. "And being I do so desire to remain in your good graces, brother, I shall be forthcoming with what I know."

Tyr gave a curt nod. Loki, having greedily taken a seat, continued to smile like a cat playing with its food. "Do tell us what you know, oh innocent lamb."

"Loki, this is not the time for your grudges." Tyr cut them off, and Loki leaned back in their chair, sulking.

Jesus nodded thanks to Tyr. "That note was given to me, amongst a few other deities. Who was it that gave it to me... Osiris, yes, that strange god. He did not say anything, and it was almost by sleight of hand that I found the note in my hand before I could even question his intent. He winked before disappearing back into the dining hall. But do not waste your time on that one, I feel he is not the source of it. Do not ask me why, I just... It's not his realm, fully." Jesus stopped for a moment, chewing on his next words. No, you'll need to find the viper's head: Persephone.

Tyr's stared, not even blinking, awaiting more.

"Ahem, yes, then what is this flower? Well, for you, and most other gods, it would just be a pleasant little glamour, just an aesthetic magic effect. But for gods related to... Rebirth, shall we say, it becomes so much more. You, being who you are Tyr, are closed off to it."

"What do you mean by that?" Tyr asked.

"You see death and duty as a final thing, as an end to things. Most gods do, you see, it's just the more... typical response to it all. But some of us, quite obviously, view it differently. We see it as a cycle.

"It spoke to me of rejuvenation, brother. You must feel it in the air? The stagnation that flitters around us like dusty moths, chewing holes in the fabrics of our minds. We sit and stew and rot in still waters and act as if it is *life*. I felt the first half of the missive deeply, brother, make no mistake. But the second half disturbed me. You know me and you know I will not lie. It spoke of a way to bring about rebirth, to bring us back to our glory, to bring vigor back into our veins. It was a simple logical statement, too: how did the mortals bring rain to their crops in dire times? Sacrifice. The bled themselves to us, killed and were killed in our names. They offered us a death to bring them life again."

"You can't seriously mean that Aphrodite was..." Tyr stammered.

"Sacrificed, brother." Loki completed the thought.

Jesus raised his eyebrow, looking both the other gods up and down, his eyes filled with a deep sorrow. "And I unfortunately see that she was... Correct on that. Know that this sickens me too, brother. This is *not* my way, not our way. We moved well past that ages ago. But it seems that in desperate times, radical seeds find welcome soil. We are dying, but to bring about death of our last kin just to bring us life again is not..." Jesus spat the last phrase, seeming unable to finish it. A rare sign of anger in the placid god.

"You said not to pursue Osiris brother..." Loki chimed in.

"Ahh, yes, well... How do I say this? I feel he is not the one in charge... No, you'll need to find the viper's head: Persephone.

Tyr rose, "Thank you, brother. This information brings light to darkness, and while I hope it is incorrect I fear it is not."

Loki rose next, a complex soup of emotions across their face, but they said nothing to the Lamb of God as a parting gift.

"Before you two leave, be warned. This group is not a few wayward souls, stray dogs yipping loudly to make a ruckus. You are entering the lion's den and, believe it not, I would much rather see the two of you again. Perhaps at that point, Tyr, you could lecture me a bit more on the finer points of *retributive* justice, hmmm?" Jesus smirked deviously, before turning back to his previous project of assembling a wooden stool.

"Where do you think he puts all those stupid stools?" Loki mused on their way out.

***

"SO LET ME JUST GET THIS *COMPLICATED* PLAN OF YOURS CLEAR: you're going in, alone, to confront the head of a grand cult set on sacrificing us off one by one to siphon themselves a few more centuries in a twisted, despondent future. Alone. Again, brother, I stress that last part." Loki sputtered as the two marched endlessly. The walls shifted again and again, idling through varying scenes.

Tyr smiled. "No sibling, I plan to go in there with you. Two is not alone."

"Oh, right, of course, how could I forget that *tiny* detail that *I* get to die too. Fantastic. Truly brother, you astound me." Loki shook their head, which now rested on a bearded man, short cropped black hair, dark and broody.

Tyr could barely hear his sibling. His ears pumped with blood, veins filled with adrenaline. His invisible hand itched, as he tensed and loosened his functioning arm. Finally, a purpose, a clear enemy, a confrontation.

"Loki, think about the situation we find ourselves in. How deep and integrated into our siblings is this cult? Who can I trust? Guan Yu could be in with this cult for all we know. Heimdall, Ares? We do

244

not know who amongst us will betray us. Other than you and I, I cannot trust anyone in the Halls as it is. We must act now, too, so that we can have the slightest of advantage in catching them off guard. Perhaps before they can strike and murder again."

"Mortals below, I hate when *you* make sense. Fine. But I swear, if this kills me, I *will* find a way back to life just to kill you. You hear me?"

"You assume I would let you die before myself, sibling? You wound me." Tyr smiled.

Loki shook their head, but smiled in return. "I will miss you brother when we both die. Think the Universe is so kind to have made us gods an afterlife?"

"I do not intend to find out today, sibling."

With a smirk, Loki nodded their head. "Neither I, brother. And I think I might have just the final trick up my sleeve for the occasion..."

***

TYR STEELED HIMSELF TO MANY POSSIBILITIES upon his election. Confronting a god murderer was not one he imagined, but similar grave calls to justice he had rehearsed in his head again and again. He did not, however, picture confronting his first murderer to involve so many... flowers.

The outer door of Persephone's realm was beautiful and haunting now. It was an old kind of stonework, with a creeping vine that wound its way amongst the gaps between stones, perfectly without causing any damage. The vine itself blossomed and bloomed, starting from its earliest little green buds on the left side, into captivating, fully in-bloom flowers over the apex of the doorway, to slowly wilting, dying, bloated things that barely hung onto the vine near the base on the right side.

The door opened to Tyr's request, revealing a scene of beauty of Old Earth, with all the cycles of nature that once ruled the lives of mortals. Trees that had naked branches slowly budding, full, bountiful boughs of thick wood and dense leaves soaking up an invisible, eternal sun, only to turn to deep auburns and russet browns, falling to the ground, to start over once again. On the ground, mushrooms bloomed and fallen trees decomposed, weeds grew and died with the seasons, animals scurrying about in an endless cycle of preparation and rest.

"Persephone," Tyr spoke.

Persephone seemed to materialize from the dense life, stepping forward with the utmost of graces. She was lithe, with hair flowing down her back in deep, auburn curls. Her skin was sun-kissed bronze and she seemed alive and hearty, the wrinkles that had once crept into the corners of her eyes and lips having retreated.

"Brother Tyr! Sibling Loki! You *finally* found your way here, hmmm? Took the scenic route perhaps, I can't much blame you for taking in all the new life and vigor in our halls! But how unlike you to be tardy, Tyr? Tut tut. You seem so hardy, too. How curious, don't you think?" She smiled, a wicked grin like a scythe before a crop.

"Don't act so flippant, sister."

Persephone tilted her head as she spoke, "But why not, brother Tyr? Is this not the solution we have been yearning for? A way to repair the damage left by the abandonment of our humans? Why, the fact that the halls are not bursting with *celebration* at this point is a bit insulting, if I'm being honest."

Tyr took a step over the threshold, entering fully into Persephone's domain. While he did not need express consent to enter, he had, dutifully, waited for it to be extended. It had not been granted, and while Loki stood shyly at the door, Tyr had no time for pleasantries with a murderer.

"Celebrating the murder of a fellow god is not something one should expect."

"*Murder*? Mortals below, are we still going to call it that? A noble sacrifice is the way I prefer to think of it. Besides... Oh dear, Loki do come in, please, you look like a rain drenched puppy left at my door!"

Loki stepped over the threshold, a gloomy cloud behind Tyr.

"Don't look so dour dear, it's really not becoming of you. I have enough brooding in my life with Hades." She laughed. The other two gods did not. "Where was I? Yes. You condemn me, brother, I can see that already, and yet you do not challenge your own beliefs? What are you professing we do in the face of our own deaths? Sit, locked up in this place like a tomb, and try to lose ourselves in merry making and love?" Her face darkened now, the sickening smile sharpening, her face shadowed and menacing.

"What do you mean? We are not locked in a tomb, sister, this is just our new..." Tyr broke off.

"Our new what? Normal? Life? You truly cannot think us gods would go from immortality to mortality and be *fine* with it? Ohh mortals below, you *do* think that?" Her laughter bounded off the walls, echoing. "I get it, Tyr, I truly do. You may not think I am sympathetic to you, but I truly am. You're so... Rigid. And in the strongest of storms, that can be your strength. Or your undoing. As a leader it has been... Shall we say, not so much your undoing, but my ascent?

"Oh do not look so surprised! Did you really think we were all comfortable with your edicts? Your self-righteousness as you paraded around the halls so stoically? That may suit you, but it is not *our* way. No, we need to grow, we need change, we need rebirth and a cycle and freshness. Why would you deny us our right, there?"

"Do not preach to me of rights, sister. You slaughtered kin in the name of your own selfish gains! Faced with your duty and this is your answer? The cowardice," Tyr growled, ghost hand itching.

"Cowardice? Is that what we call the only one trying to better their siblings' lives now? Mortals below, the arrogance of your words. You think your status as Elected makes you unquestionable,

Tyr?"

"No. But it does make me arbiter in all matters of our kin, sister. You forget your place time and time again."

Her arms extended, like a great bird of prey, as she spun around her realm, proclaiming, "Quite the opposite! I am well aware of my place as one intimately attuned to the need for rebirth in *all* things. Yes, sacrifices must be made. For the betterment of all!"

"Murder chosen by you, by your hands, without consent."

Persephone smiled, approaching Tyr, "Chosen by *my* hands? Truly, Tyr, you are so narrow in your scope. Do you think I acted alone? That I am the only one moving to activate our great ideals here? Cut my head, and see how large the hydra that *hungers* for regrowth is."

"Ohhh, I see, you've created a democracy to say who'll get the ax next then, sister?" Loki broke their silence, anger creeping through their lips.

"Mmm, in a way. More of a council. Leaving it up to the election, well, that didn't work so well the first time it seems." She gestured towards Tyr, who bristled.

Loki took steps towards Persephone, who seemed to welcome him with her extended arms. "And this... Council's decisions, are they included on the list of possible sacrifices then?"

"Of course. We are nothing if not fair in who might be next under the blade. Besides, if our theories are anything to go off of, we shouldn't need to be making another sacrifice for another century or two. We wonder if a younger, stronger god's death might prolong that but, well, none really fit that category!" She laughed again, smiling.

"Question is, whether next time will even extend that too then, no? What with us all being on death's door anyways, bit hard to find good specimens. But next time… That will be interesting then, no?"

"Yes, we're not twisted though. We're curious but not excited about the next sacrifice. But the results from this one alone… Surely, as I am already sensing, the gods will see the reason in our actions! What is the cost of one of our lives to prolong the whole?"

"To keep a tree healthy, you have to prune away some branches…"

Tyr looked at his sibling aghast. "Sibling, you cannot be swayed by this madness!"

Loki pushed past Tyr in this moment. "Silence, Tyr. Mortals below I've had enough of *waiting* for my death to come to me. Let me at least listen."

"See, Tyr! Even your own accomplice sees the light of our reasoning! We are gods, what are we if we simply succumb to mortality without at least trying to outwit it? I figured you would be sympathetic to that, Loki. I'm glad I was not wrong."

Tyr shook with rage at the sight before him. Betrayal, he had expected, but he felt he could at least trust Loki. He thought they had changed from their conniving way… His blood boiled. "Traitorous cur! You would throw the rest of us under the knife for a few more years of life! Sacrifice our own codes for a few scraps of a twisted, macabre years!"

Approaching Loki now too, arms extended as if to embrace a prodigal child, Persephone spoke, "Ignore him, sibling. You know how the dogs will yelp while wolves act."

Loki barked a laugh, "Sister, I've been ignoring that one for years uncountable."

The scene shifted rapidly in the span of the next few moments. At Loki's approach, Persephone stood, arms still wide, as if to embrace the trickster god. Her eyes, shining with the brightness of victory, were blind to the deceit.

From around Loki's own waist, where once a simple leather belt had been, appeared a glowing, rune covered links of a chain. It hummed with dwarven magics, and the predator smile on Persephone's face shifted to the doe eyes of prey. In their right hand they held this chain, which wrapped itself like a friendly serpent along Loki's arm; in their left hand they drew a short, dark iron dagger.

Recognition played a tempest storm across Persephone's face. "L-Loki you can't surely mean to…"

Loki tut-tutted her, before extending their arm with the Gleipnir towards the flowery goddess. It wound its way along her body, moving quickly to constrain her legs and next her arms. Her mouth opened to protest, but Loki, having closed the distance in the blink of an eye, held the angry, burning dagger against her neck.

"Now now sister, truly, please shut up."

"You idiotic, weak willed, bastardiz--" Persephone protested, before Gleipnir, having woven its way along her arms, conveniently made a gag across her mouth.

Loki sighed, a deep, heavy thing, before turning towards Tyr. "Mortals below, well done brother! That performance had me moved! But, of course, I knew you to be an *awful* actor. Sorry for that moment of mistrust, brother, truly." They bowed before Tyr, the tip of their dagger never leaving the throat of Persephone all the while.

Tyr stammered, tongue still trying to form words to express his emotions.

They laughed, moving away from the bound Persephone, who glared daggers at the two gods. "Here I was thinking *you* were the most preachy of the gods on ethics at times, brother! I retract that. How *long* was she going to go on?"

"Sibling... Thank you." Tyr strode forward, wrapping meaty arms around his sibling.

"You... You're... Wel... Brother... Breath... I..."

Tyr let go, laughing a laugh that felt sweet as it escaped his lips. "I knew you said you had a trick, sibling, but could you have not at least *warned* me it involved acting out betrayal?"

"And rely on your crude acting abilities, brother? Mortals below, you never did have many *artists* pray to you, did you? Besides, a trickster has to have *a little fun*, and my oh my was your face priceless! Truly though, do you have such a low view of me that you would actually believe I'd leave you for *that* sorry lot?" At this, Loki gestured their head back towards Persephone, who writhed in response.

Tyr laughed, shaking his head. "Quite the opposite, sibling. It stung all the more because I *do* trust you now. It is… A strange feeling, to be sure." He smiled, feeling of a weight off his shoulders, like a rock rolled away, for the first time in decades.

Then, as soon as the relief had come, it left.

"There's… More of them though, she said. She may not even be their leader entirely. And while they won't need to act for many years we have to be prepared to act again, it would seem, sibling. Never thought it'd be you I leaned on in my hour of need, nor to call upon you again when the time comes." Tyr smiled wearily at his sibling.

"Makes two of us, brother. Now, what are we to do with this hydra?"

"We have another lead to follow up on: Osiris. Weeding out who amongst our ranks is aligned with this cultish group, who we can count on amongst our own… But first, I believe a trial is in order. It has been so long since I've had that pleasure." Tyr smiled a wolfish grin towards the gagged goddess.

About The Editor

JULIA T. LYE is a graduate of Carleton University living in Ottawa as she pursues a career in creative writing. Her short stories have been published in the horror anthology 'What Lies in Wait', the science fiction anthology 'The Stranger Side of Tomorrow', and the romance anthology 'You Hit Me with Your Car (and Other Love Stories)', and her debut novel, 'Anelisha Knight in the Yarns of Gods', was published by DeeBee Books in May of 2019. When she isn't tapping away at her keyboard, she likes to run original Dungeons and Dragons campaigns, read any book she can get her hands on, and create digital art. Julia is also one of the instructors with the Ottawa Writing Workshops. You can reach her at lyejulia@gmail.com or check out her website at www.julialye.com

Acknowledgments

This collection of short stories would not have been possible without the energy and enthusiasm of the Ottawa Workshop writers who contributed their talents to it. This collection was compiled and designed by Léa Marshall-Raymond.

Thanks for reading! If you enjoyed this collection, please add a short review on Amazon and/or Goodreads.

Reviews mean a lot to writers, so I encourage you to support our growing writers' community by taking a few minutes now to rate this collection and write a few words of encouragement about it. And please share your copy of the book with others!